LIFE

The World of Plants

1:1
Answers
IN GENESIS™

GOD'S
DESIGN®

4th Edition
Debbie & Richard Lawrence

God's Design® for Life is a complete life science curriculum for grades 3–8. The books in this series are designed for use in the Christian school and homeschool, and provide easy-to-use lessons that will encourage children to see God's hand in everything around them.

Printed January 2016

Fourth edition. Copyright © 2003, 2008, 2016 by Debbie & Richard Lawrence.

ISBN: 978-1-62691-424-7

Published by Answers in Genesis, 2800 Bullittsburg Church Rd., Petersburg KY 41080

Book design: Diane King
Editor: Gary Vaterlaus

The publisher and authors have made every reasonable effort to ensure that the activities recommended in this book are safe when performed as instructed but assume no responsibility for any damage caused or sustained while conducting the experiments and activities. It is the parents', guardians', and/or teachers' responsibility to supervise all recommended activities.

Printed in China

Welcome to GOD'S DESIGN®

LIFE

You are about to start an exciting series of lessons on life science. *God's Design® for Life* consists of three books: *The World of Plants*, *The World of Animals*, and *The Human Body*. Each of these books will give you insight into how God designed and created our world and the things that live in it.

No matter what grade you are in, third through eighth grade, you can use this book.

3rd–5th grade

Read the lesson.

 Do the activity in the light blue box (worksheets will be provided by your teacher).

 Test your knowledge by answering the **What did we learn?** questions.

 Assess your understanding by answering the **Taking it further** questions.

Be sure to read the special features and do the final project.

There are also unit quizzes and a final test to take.

6th–8th grade

Read the lesson.

 Do the activity in the light blue box (worksheets will be provided by your teacher).

 Test your knowledge by answering the **What did we learn?** questions.

 Assess your understanding by answering the **Taking it further** questions.

 Do the challenge section in the light green box. This part of the lesson will challenge you to do more advanced activities and learn additional interesting information.

Be sure to read the special features and do the final project.

There are also unit quizzes and a final test to take.

When you truly understand how God has designed everything in our universe to work together, then you will enjoy the world around you even more. So let's get started!

UNIT 1

Introduction to Life Science

◊ **Identify** the six characteristics of living things.

◊ **Identify** the five kingdoms of living things.

◊ **Identify** the method of classification of living things.

◊ **Describe** the need for scientific names.

◊ **Describe** basic parts of a cell using models.

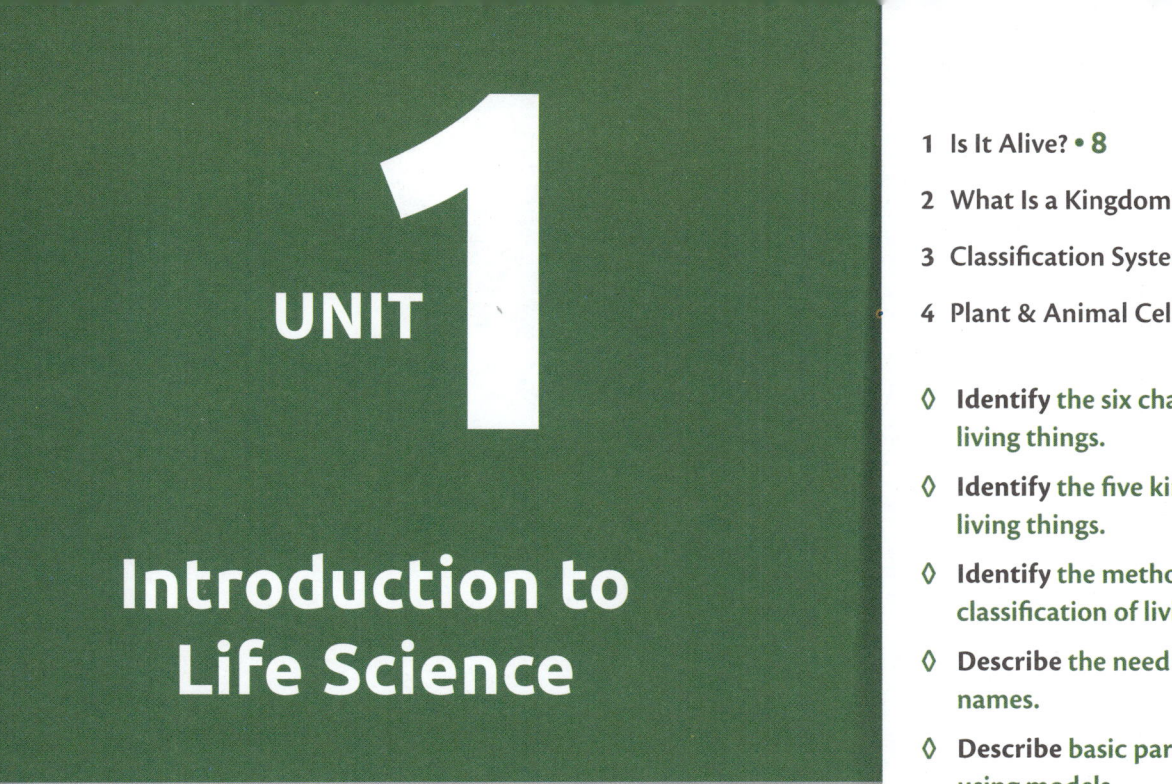

1

Is It Alive?

Biology is the study of living things.

How do we know if something is alive?

Words to know:

respiration

Challenge words:

spontaneous generation   abiogenesis

law of biogenesis   chemical evolution

How can we tell if something is alive? Look at the things around you. Is an animal alive? Is a plant alive? Is the table alive? How about your computer? Some things are obviously alive while other things are obviously not alive. Still other things might be a little more confusing. We are getting ready to study plants, and the study of plants is part of the study of life science. Before we can study life science, we need to know what is considered alive scientifically and what is not. It will help you to identify living things if you realize that all living things have six common characteristics:

1. Living things eat or absorb nutrients. All living things need food and water. Most animals take in food and water through their mouths. Plants absorb nutrients from the soil through their roots.

2. Living things perform **respiration**—they "breathe" or exchange oxygen and carbon dioxide as they turn food into energy. Both plants and animals need oxygen to survive. Animals get oxygen from their surroundings in many different ways. We are most familiar with animals that breathe with lungs. But some animals, such as fish, breathe with gills, and others, such as Earthworms, can absorb

oxygen through their skin. Plants also "breathe" by exchanging carbon dioxide and oxygen through their leaves. During the day, when sunlight is abundant, plants use carbon dioxide to produce food through photosynthesis; however, at night, plants use oxygen to break down some of that food for energy to grow. The type of respiration performed by all living things is called cellular respiration. It involves using oxygen to break down sugars to release energy needed for the processes of life. Different processes are used to exchange the gases required for and produced by cellular respiration—how it "breathes"—but all organisms use energy.

3. Living things grow. All plants and animals have a life cycle in which they are born, develop and grow, and then die.

4. Living things reproduce. Animals and plants reproduce in many different ways, but God designed each living thing to be able to produce more of its own kind. Most animals have babies and most plants produce seeds, but there are other ways of reproducing such as dividing or producing spores.

5. Living things move and respond to their environment. Animals can move in many different ways: some run, some fly, some slither, some swim. Plants can't move around like animals but they do respond to their environment. Plants turn their leaves to face the sun. Their roots grow down and their stems grow up. Many flowers close at night and open in the morning. This is their way of moving and responding.

6. Living things have cells. Even though we can't see plant and animal cells without the aid of a microscope, we know that all living things are made up of living cells.

Are Plants Alive Biblically?

When we talk about the study of living things from a scientific perspective, we use a definition of living things that is based on what we can observe about the organism God has created. But, according to the Bible, there is a difference between plant life and animal and human life. Throughout the Bible, the Hebrew words *nephesh chayyâh* are used to describe human and animal life. When referring to mankind, *nephesh chayyâh* means "living soul" or "soulish creature," and when it refers to animals, it means "living creature." However, this word is never applied to plant life. There is a plain distinction. It is easy to see that plants do not experience pain, suffering, or death in the same way that humans and animals do. Plant death is not the death of a "living soul" or "living creature."

As you consider the six characteristics above, keep in mind that we are using the scientific definition of a living thing. To see a biblical example of the distinction, read the following passages and compare how they talk about humans or animals and plants: Genesis 2:7, 6:17, 7:15, 7:22; Leviticus 17:10–12; Psalm 104:24–30; Matthew 6:25–34.

What did we learn?

- What are the six questions you should ask to determine if something is biologically alive?
- Does the Bible refer to plants as living things?

Taking it further

- Do scientists consider a piece of wood that has been cut off of a tree living? (Hint: Is it growing? Can it respond?)
- Is paper alive?
- Is a seed alive?

Is it alive? scavenger hunt

Use a copy of the "Is it Alive? Scavenger Hunt" worksheet to determine whether items inside and outside of your house are alive or not.

Law of biogenesis

Now that you know how to determine if something is alive, you understand that living things come from living things. An apple tree produces seeds that grow into new apple trees; a dog gives birth to puppies that grow up to be dogs. This observation is completely consistent with the Bible when it says in Genesis that plants and animals were created to reproduce after their own kind. Also, in Matthew chapter 7, Jesus said that people could tell a plant by its fruit—a thorn bush does not produce grapes and a thistle plant does not produce figs. Today, scientists better understand plant and animal reproduction and realize that DNA in the cells determines what kind of plant or animal will be produced.

However, people did not always understand that living things must come from living things. At one time, people thought that rats were produced by garbage because they observed that rats were more abundant when there was more garbage. People also thought that rotting meat produced maggots, which grow into flies, because they observed that when meat was left to rot, maggots often appeared within a few days. This idea is called spontaneous generation. People believed that these animals were somehow suddenly produced by their surroundings. It took the

work of a some very persistent scientists to dispel this idea.

In about 1665 an Italian scientist named Francesco Redi did several experiments to show that spontaneous generation did not occur. He believed that maggots came from flies, not from rotting meat. To prove this he put some meat into three different jars. The first jar was left open to the air. The second jar was covered with a layer of gauze which allowed air to pass through. The third jar was covered with a thick parchment that prevented anything from passing into or out of the jar. What do you think happened in each of the three jars?

In the first jar maggots appeared in a few days, just as people had seen before. In the second jar, eggs and later maggots were found on top of the gauze, but no maggots were found inside the jar. There were no eggs, maggots, or flies in or around the third jar. This experiment showed that the maggots came from eggs that were laid by flies which were attracted by the smell of the decomposing meat. When the jar was sealed the flies did not smell the meat and did not lay their eggs, so there were no maggots. This experiment did much to dispel the idea of spontaneous generation; however, many people still believed that simple organisms such as bacteria might still be produced without parents.

In the 1800s Louis Pasteur worked to show that even simple organisms such as bacteria only come from other bacteria. Pasteur experimented with different samples of broth. He showed that bacteria freely reproduced in an open container of broth. He then boiled the broth to kill all of the bacteria. Some of this broth was exposed to the air and other broth was kept in a sealed container. The broth exposed to the air developed new bacteria but the sealed jar did not. Pasteur believed that bacteria were entering the jar on dust particles in the air. To show that this was true, he created a bottle with a zigzag neck that allowed air to enter but prevented dust and other particles from entering the jar. The broth in this jar did not develop any bacteria even after four years. In fact, even after 100 years, no bacteria were found in this jar, which is now on display in the Pasteur Institute in Paris. Pasteur's experiments laid to rest the idea of spontaneous generation.

Louis Pasteur

These experiments proved that life only comes from other life. This is such an important idea that it is called the **law of biogenesis**. Every experiment has shown that in order to get something that is alive, you must start with one or more living things and that you always get what you started with. Bacteria produce bacteria, flies produce flies, and people produce people. This is exactly how God designed the world to work.

Despite the fact that biogenesis is what we always observe, many scientists today believe that at one time life came from nonlife. They refer to this occurrence as **abiogenesis** or **chemical evolution**. These scientists believe that many millions of years ago under just the right circumstances, chemicals accidentally combined to form proteins, which are the building blocks of living cells, and that these proteins combined to form simple living creatures. Scientists have even tried to reproduce this event in the laboratory; however, even with a very controlled environment, no one has ever built living cells from just chemicals. Even if they could produce life in a lab, all it would prove is that intelligence can produce life. It would not prove that life can evolve from chemicals on its own.

God's Word is true, and as you learn more about living things, you will be amazed at how beautifully God designed each living thing to reproduce to continue the cycle of life.

2

What Is a Kingdom?

It's alive, but what is it?

How are plants different from animals?

Words to know:

taxonomy	anatomy
zoology	kingdom
botany	

Challenge words:

dichotomous key

Once we determine that something is alive, how do we tell what it is? Scientists have grappled with this question for centuries. Carl Linnaeus is credited with developing the method of classification, or **taxonomy**, that we use today. But that classification system has been modified over the centuries to reflect new understanding of the living world.

The study of living things can be divided into three broad categories. The study of animals is called **zoology** while the study of plants is called **botany**. We use the word **anatomy** to talk about the different parts of plants, animals, or humans. But as scientists have learned more about the world of living things that God created, they have discovered that not everything fits neatly into plants or animals.

One system divides all living things into five kingdoms. A **kingdom** is a group of living things that has broad common characteristics.

The first two kingdoms are *plants*, which include all green plants that perform photosynthesis, and *fungi*, which cannot make their own food. The final three kingdoms are *animals*, which are multi-celled creatures, *protists*, which are single- and multi-celled creatures, and *monerans*, which are bacteria. Some scientists divide the kingdom Monera into two groups (Eubacteria and Archaea) based on their differing characteristics. For simplicity, we are going to treat them as one kingdom.

Because most protists and monerans are microscopic, plants and animals are the living things that most people recognize. To separate living things into different kingdoms, we must look at what is the same and what is different, and then sort them based on their differences. By answering the following questions, we can begin to determine whether a living thing is a plant or an animal.

For both plants and animals:

- Is it alive? All plants and animals are alive.

- Does it have cells? All plants and animals have cells.

- Does it reproduce after its own kind? God created

all plants and animals with the ability to make more plants and animals just like themselves.

- Does it need oxygen? All plants and animals need oxygen. We will see that the way they obtain that oxygen can be very different from one living thing to another, but they all use it.

- Do they demonstrate God's design? All plants and animals are special and created just the way God wanted them to be. You will see this great master plan as you study the plants and animals in more detail.

For plants only:

- Do the cells have chlorophyll? Chlorophyll is what makes leaves green. Plants have it; animals don't.

Fun Fact

Did you know that plants were created before there was even a sun? According to Genesis chapter 1 plants were created on Day Three of creation, and the sun, moon, and stars were created on Day Four. The plants could not have survived very long if the sun had not been created the next day.

- Does it make its own food? Plants use chlorophyll to change the sun's energy into food for the plant. Animals cannot do this and must eat either plants or other animals that eat plants.

- Does it need the sun to survive? Many animals live in places that receive little or no sunshine. But all green plants must have sunshine to make food.

- Do they need carbon dioxide? Plants use carbon dioxide in photosynthesis when they make food. Animals do not need carbon dioxide. It is a waste product that they must get rid of.

For animals only:

- Can it move about freely? Although plants and animals both move in some sense, animals move about freely in their environment. Plants are rooted to the ground and therefore cannot move from one place to another.

Plants are different from animals because plants can produce their own food using carbon dioxide, chlorophyll, and the sun. Also, plants are limited in their movement. Animals, on the other hand, move freely, but must eat plants or other animals for food.

Animal or plant game

Purpose: To play a game as you identify the characteristics of plants and animals

Materials: "Clue Cards" handout, poster board, pen, scissors

Procedure:

1. Divide a piece of poster board into three sections as shown here. Label the left column *Animals*, the right column *Plants*, and the center section a few inches up from the bottom *Both*.

   Animals   Plants

                        Both

2. Cut out the clue cards, mix them up, and place them face down on the table.

3. Have a person draw the first card and place it in the correct column. If the card describes a characteristic of plants only put it in the *Plants* column, if it describes only animals put it in the *Animals* column. If it describes both plants and animals put it in the *Both* column.

4. Have the next person draw the next card and so on. If someone has difficulty choosing the correct column, review the questions in this lesson or let the others help.

🧠 What did we learn?

- What do plants and animals have in common?
- What makes plants unique?
- What makes animals unique?

🚀 Taking it further

- Are mushrooms plants?
- Why do you think they are or are not?

🏅 Dichotomous key

When scientists try to identify a living organism, they often use charts that have been developed by careful observation. These charts begin with two questions or options that describe a particular characteristic that helps divide the organisms into two groups. Based on the answer to the first question, the chart then presents two new questions/options to further help identify characteristics of the organism. Because there are always two possible answers, the chart is called a **dichotomous key**. To see how this works, use the dichotomous keys below to help you identify the animals and plants that are shown. Choose one of the plants or animals listed at the bottom of the chart. We will use the cat for our

example. Go to the top of the chart and ask yourself the question, "Does this animal have a backbone or no backbone?" It has a backbone, so you follow that branch of the chart. The next question is, "Is this animal warm-blooded or cold-blooded?" The cat is warm-blooded so you move down that branch. Finally ask, "Does this animal have hair or feathers?" The cat has hair so you follow that branch and identify the animal as a cat. Follow the branch for each plant and animal on each chart. It is okay if you do not know the answers for every question for every example. This will still give you an idea of how these charts work. These charts are very simple compared to the detailed charts used by scientists.

Animal Identification Key

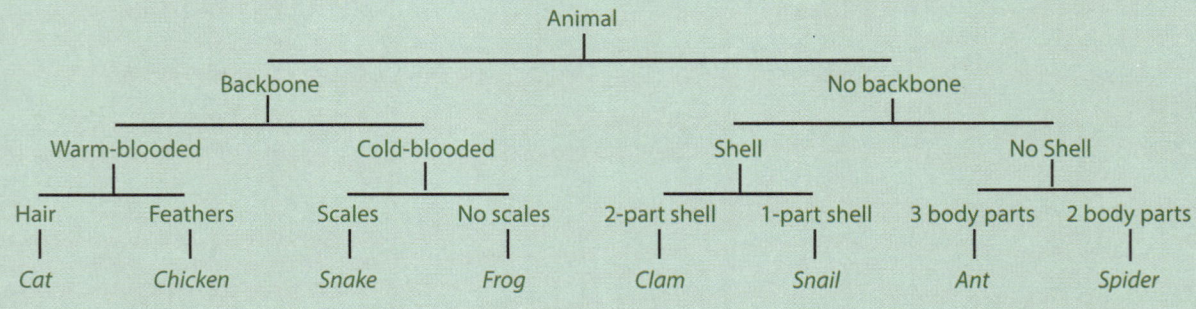

Plant/Leaf Identification Key

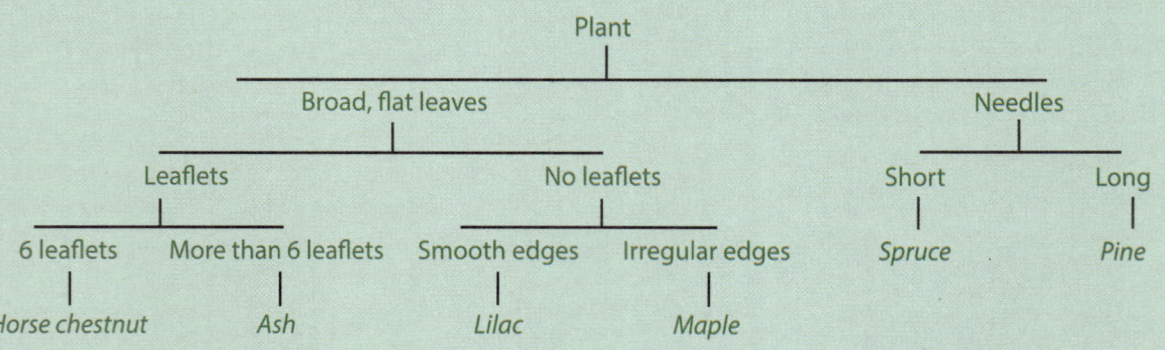

3

Classification System

Taxonomy—classification of living things

How are living things classified?

Words to know:

phylum	family
vascular tissue	genus
class	species
order	binomial classification

Determining if something is a plant or an animal is just the beginning of classification. One modern classification system uses a seven-level method for describing what something is. The top level is the kingdom. As we learned in the last lesson, there are five kingdoms recognized today: plants, animals, fungi, protists, and monerans. Once a specimen is determined to fit into one of these kingdoms, it is then placed into a **phylum** (FI-lum). A phylum (plural: phyla) separates the specimens in a kingdom by common characteristics. For example, animals are separated into a phylum based on whether they have a backbone or not—vertebrates and invertebrates. One of the characteristics used to divide plants into phyla is whether or not they have **vascular tissue**, a series of tubes to carry nutrients throughout the plant.

Each phylum is then divided into classes—again according to common characteristics. Each **class** is divided into orders. Each **order** is divided into families. A **family** is divided into genera (plural of genus). And each **genus** is divided into **species**. This may seem complicated, but a couple of examples should help you understand how this works.

The strawberry plant is classified below:

Kingdom	Plant	
Phylum	Tracheophyta	Has vascular tissue
Class	Angiosperm	Reproduces with flowers, fruits, and seeds
Order	Rosales	Flower grows from beneath ovary
Family	Rosaceae	Flowers grow up to four inches wide
Genus	*Fragaria*	Leaves grow in groups of three
Species	*vesca*	Strawberry

Now let's look at an example of an animal classification. Your pet dog is classified below:

Kingdom	Animal	
Phylum	Vertebrate	Has a backbone
Class	Mammal	Has hair, nurses young, warm-blooded
Order	Carnivore	Flesh-eating
Family	Canidae	Dog-like
Genus	*Canis*	Dog
Species	*familiaris*	Domestic

Fun Fact

Mountain lion, cougar, catamount, wildcat, and puma all refer to the same animal, depending on where you live. So it's a good thing that scientists use Latin names, like *Puma concolor*, to describe living things to avoid confusion.

Generally, a living thing is identified by its Latin genus and species names. For example, the family dog would be identified as a *canis familiaris*. This **binomial**, or two-name, **classification** system was adopted by Carl Linnaeus in the 18th century and is still used today to help scientists easily identify what they are talking about. Common names are not used for scientific purposes because the common name can be different from one area to another or even from one person to another. For example, one group of people might call a plant a chickpea plant and another group might call it a garbanzo bean plant. So using the Latin names helps avoid confusion.

Dividing plants and animals into this classification system can be subjective. And scientists do not always agree on where a creature or plant should be placed. Also, some modern scientists are attempting to change the classifications to reflect supposed evolutionary chains. There is no evidence for these evolutionary classifications, and good scientists use what can be observed and tested to make good conclusions.

Finally, when evolutionists talk about one animal evolving into another, they are referring to one kind of creature or plant changing into another. For example, they say that dogs, bears, seals, and raccoons all came from a common weasel-like ancestor millions of years ago. But what we actually observe is that dogs reproduce dogs, bears make bears, etc. Some wild dogs such as wolves and domestic dogs can interbreed. They came from a common dog kind that was on the Ark and survived the Flood. But a dog is still a dog, and a cat is still a cat.

What did we learn?

- What are the five kingdoms recognized today?
- How do scientists determine how to classify a living thing?
- What are the seven levels of the classification system?

Taking it further

- Why can pet dogs breed with wild wolves?
- How many of each animal kind did Noah take on the Ark?

Remembering the system

You can memorize one of the following sayings to help remember the classification system:

Keep	Penguins	Cool	Or	Find	Good	Shelter
Kings	Play	Chess	On	Fine	Green	Squares
(**K**ingdom	**P**hylum	**C**lass	**O**rder	**F**amily	**G**enus	**S**pecies)

Look up the classification for some of your favorite plants or animals in a reference guide or on the Internet.

🏅 Plant classification

You will be able to understand plants better if you understand how scientists classify plants. First, plants are divided into two groups: plants with vascular tissue and plants without vascular tissue. Plants are further divided based primarily on how they reproduce.

Plants with vascular tissue have a series of tubes throughout the plant. These tubes function very much like the blood vessels in a human. They carry nutrients throughout the plants. Whether a plant has vascular tissue or not determines which phylum the plant belongs to.

Nonvascular plants are divided into three groups: mosses, liverworts, and hornworts. Together these are called bryophytes. These nonvascular plants have leaves and stems, but do not have true roots. They reproduce by spores, not with flowers. The bryophytes tend to grow in clumps in moist areas. You may find them growing on tree trunks or along streams, but don't confuse them with the algae growing in the water. Even though algae contain chlorophyll, they are not plants since they do not have leaves, stems, and roots.

Vascular plants are divided into two subphyla: plants that produce seeds and plants that do not produce seeds. Seedless plants reproduce using spores. These plants include horsetails, ferns, and club mosses.

Vascular plants with seeds are further divided into two classes: gymnosperms and angiosperms. Gymnosperms are plants that produce seeds that are not enclosed in fruit. These plants

Ginkgo tree

primarily reproduce with seeds that form in cones. Angiosperms are plants that produce seeds that are enclosed in fruit.

There are three main groups of gymnosperms. The largest group is the conifers. These plants have needle-like or scaly leaves and have the cones that we are familiar with such as pine cones or spruce cones. The second group of gymnosperms is the cycads (SI-kadz). These plants produce very large cones that grow out of the center of a large circle of palm tree style leaves. There are only a few species of cycads flourishing today, although many species are common in the fossil record. The sago palm is the most commonly cultivated cycad. The third group of gymnosperms is the ginkgoes. Ginkgoes have fleshy cones and unique fan-shaped leaves. Ginkgoes are native to China and are the only gymnosperms that shed their leaves. Ginkgoes are sometimes called living fossils because they were thought to be extinct, only found in the fossil record, until they were rediscovered in China.

Finally, angiosperms are divided into two main sub-classes based on the types of seed that the plant produces. Plants that produce two-part seeds are called dicots. Plants that produce seeds with only one part are called monocots. Angiosperms are the most common types of plants. You will learn much more about these plants in the following lessons.

Now that you have learned about how the plant kingdom is divided up, take the information above and draw a key or chart similar to the dichotomous keys you used in the previous lesson.

Thallose liverwort

Carl Linnaeus

1707–1778
Father of Taxonomy

Carl Linnaeus (also known as Carolus Linnaeus) came into the world on May 23, 1707, in southern Sweden. His father Nils Linnaeus was a Lutheran pastor, as well as an avid gardener and amateur botanist, which tells you where Carl got his love of plants. His father and mother hoped he would follow in his father's footsteps and become a pastor. Carl did follow him—right out to the garden, every chance he got. By the time he was five, his father gave him his own garden to take care of. In school, Carl got the nickname of "Little Botanicus" because of his love of plants.

Carl was originally studying to become a priest, but on the advice of his teachers, Carl got permission to study medicine. At this time, every doctor had to prepare and prescribe drugs derived from plants. This move suited Carl, and in his autobiography he wrote that studying had become as much fun as it was unpleasant before.

Even though he enjoyed his studies, Carl did not go into medicine but instead spent his time giving lectures on botany. Later, he applied to the Royal Science Society in Uppsala, Sweden, and received a grant for a scientific journey to Lapland in northern Sweden. From a natural history point of view, Lapland was still unknown. In May of 1732, Carl went north and studied the plants in Lapland. Carl Linnaeus's journals were so complete that his trip to the north attracted attention from both inside and outside of Sweden.

By this time Linnaeus had started his work on grouping plants together, but not everyone agreed with him. A botanist named Johann Siegesbeck criticized his work. However, Carl did not let this bother him. He continued his work and he even named a useless European weed *Siegesbeckia* in honor of his critic. It is not certain who

got the last laugh as this weed was later found to have medicinal uses.

Through his work, Linnaeus was able to influence several students to travel as far as America in search of new plants. He also worked to find plants or crops that would grow in Sweden that could be exported in order to reduce Sweden's dependency on imports. He also tried to find native plants that could be used for tea, coffee, flour, and fodder (food for livestock), but was unsuccessful in this venture.

Carl's real claim to fame, though, is that he was the first to consistently use the two-Latin-name system (binomial) for classifying plants and animals. The first name defines the genus, or grouping of similar organisms, and the second part defines the species. For example, a human is classified as *Homo sapiens*; *Homo* meaning primate and *sapiens* meaning humanity (though we know that humans are not related to primates, such as apes).

You may wonder if Carl Linnaeus was a Christian. If you read his writings, you will see that he was. He wrote in the preface to a late edition of *Systema Naturae*, "The earth's creation is the glory of God, as seen from the works of nature by man alone."

Linnaeus did not believe in evolution. In his early years, he believed that species were unchangeable as he wrote, "The invariability of species is the condition for order in nature." He was saying that the descendants of a deer or woodpecker would be the same as the original animal.

In later years, he abandoned the concept that species were fixed and invariable and suggested that species might alter through the process of acclimatization (or adaptation). In other words, species can change to fit their environment. We see evidence of these kinds of changes. For example, moths that blend in with their environment are not eaten so they survive to reproduce whereas those that did not blend in get eaten. After a few generations, the overall color of the population has changed to fit the environment. This is not a change from one kind of animal to another kind; it is merely a change in the dominant color of the overall population.

Linnaeus did not believe that the process of change was open-ended or unlimited. One kind does not change into another kind. The moths are still moths. They did not change into a frog or some other animal. Whatever changes have occurred within a kind have arisen from the original kind that God created.

Although the system we use today to group plants and animals is somewhat different from what Carl Linnaeus used, his early work laid the foundation for what we use today. Carl Linnaeus helped us develop a way to organize what we see around us and helped direct us to the Creator of that order.

4

Plant & Animal Cells

The smallest unit of life

What are the basic parts of a cell?

Words to know:

cell	cytoplasm
organelle	cell wall
cell membrane	chloroplast
nucleus	tissue
vacuole	organ
mitochondria	

Challenge words:

mitosis	telophase
prophase	cytokinesis
metaphase	meiosis
anaphase	

You have learned that all living things are made of cells, so plants and animals have cells—but what is a cell? A **cell** is the smallest structural unit of an organism that is capable of functioning independently. Some living organisms exist only as a single cell, while an average-sized man contains from 60 to 100 trillion cells. Understanding cells helps us to understand the detail and intricacies of what God created so we can appreciate how everything works together.

Animal cells contain many specialized parts, called **organelles**. Five of these main structures are:

- **Cell membrane**—acts like the "skin" of the cell. It surrounds and protects the rest of the cell. It also recognizes other cells.

- **Nucleus**—the "brain" of the cell. It is the control center of the cell. It also contains the genetic code used to produce new cells.

- **Vacuoles**—storage "warehouses" that store food for the cell, as well as storage of waste.

- **Mitochondria**—the "power stations" of the cell. They break down the food and with the addition of oxygen produce energy for the cell.

- **Cytoplasm**—the "transportation network" of the cell. It is the liquid that fills the cell and allows all the other parts of the cell to move around inside the cell.

Animal cells can have many different shapes depending on the function of the cell, but the majority of them are round.

Plant cells have the same basic organelles as animal cells, as well as these two additional structures:

Animal cell

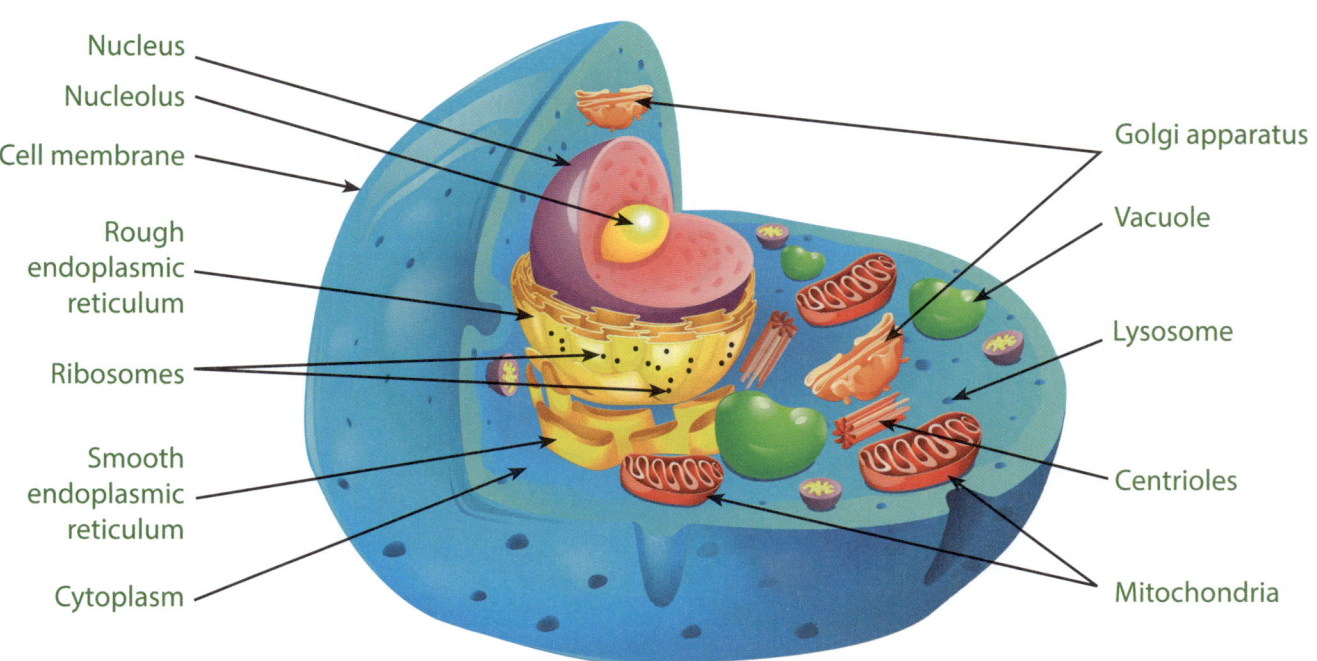

Nucleus

Nucleolus

Cell membrane

Rough endoplasmic reticulum

Ribosomes

Smooth endoplasmic reticulum

Cytoplasm

Golgi apparatus

Vacuole

Lysosome

Centrioles

Mitochondria

- **Cell wall**—provides support for the cell. It surrounds the cell membrane and gives it strength and form. This allows plants to be rigid even though they do not have a skeleton like most animals do.

- **Chloroplasts**—the "food factories" of the cell. They make sugars using water and carbon dioxide in the presence of chlorophyll and sunlight. The presence of chloroplasts is a major factor in determining if a living thing is a plant rather than an animal.

Plant cell

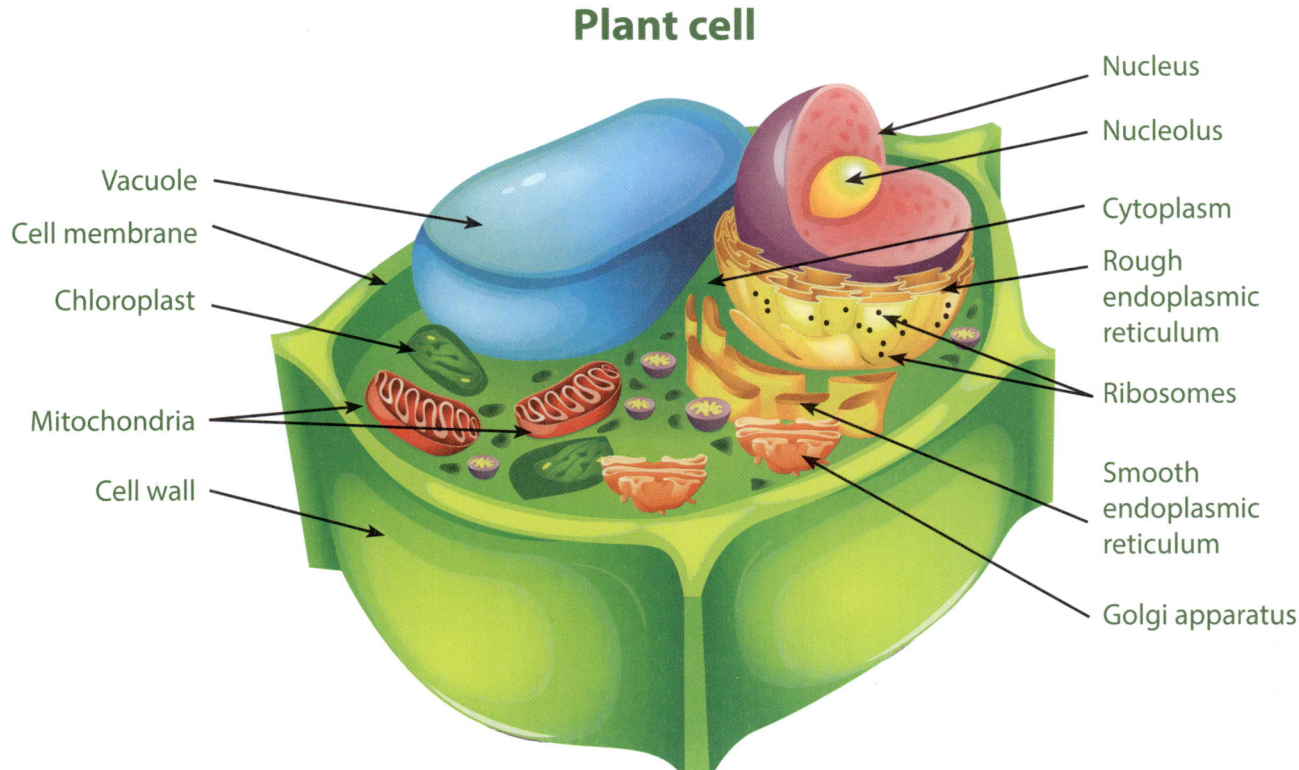

Vacuole

Cell membrane

Chloroplast

Mitochondria

Cell wall

Nucleus

Nucleolus

Cytoplasm

Rough endoplasmic reticulum

Ribosomes

Smooth endoplasmic reticulum

Golgi apparatus

Plant cells generally have a square or rectangular shape. The cell wall helps the plant cell hold its shape, which in turn helps the entire plant hold its shape.

Even though each cell can function on its own, plants and animals were designed for cells to work together with other cells. A group of cells working together to perform a function is called a **tissue**. A group of tissues working together is called an **organ**. To appreciate how small a cell is, realize that one average tree leaf has approximately 50 million cells.

What did we learn?

- What parts or structures do all plant and animal cells have?

- What structures are unique to plants?

- What distinguishes animal cells from plant cells?

Taking it further

- A euglena is a single-celled living organism that can move around by itself. It eats other creatures, but it also has chlorophyll in its cell. Is it a plant, an animal, or something else?

Other organelles

Research and write the function of these other organelles in animal and plant cells by looking them up in an encyclopedia or the Internet:

- centrioles
- ribosome
- lysosome
- golgi apparatus
- nucleolus
- smooth endoplasmic reticulum
- rough endoplasmic reticulum

Making a model of a cell

Purpose: To make a model of a cell

Option A—Construction paper model

Materials: construction paper, glue, scissors

Procedure:

1. Cut pieces of construction paper to resemble the parts of a cell (see previous pictures). Use different colors of construction paper for each part of the cell.

2. Glue them together to make a model of each kind of cell. Be sure to make a rectangular cell with a cell wall and green chloroplasts for a plant cell, and a round cell without those structures for an animal cell.

Option B—Gelatin model

Materials: gelatin, zipper bag, red grape, raisins, green grapes, shoe box

Procedure:

1. Mix the gelatin according to the box directions and place in the refrigerator for about 1 hour.

2. Fill a zipper bag about ¾ full of the thickened gelatin. The bag represents the cell membrane and the gelatin represents the cytoplasm.

3. Insert a red grape for the nucleus and several raisins for the mitochondria.

4. Squish the ingredients around to see how the parts of the cell move. If you move most of the cytoplasm away from an area, that would represent an empty space for a vacuole where food could be stored. This is your basic animal cell model.

5. To make a plant cell model, add several green grapes to represent chloroplasts.

6. Now place the bag inside a small shoe box. The sides of the box support the bag and give it strength just as the cell wall does in a plant cell.

7. To represent a tissue, stack several boxes together to make a tower.

8. You can stack more boxes together to make a bridge, pyramid, or other structure to represent an organ.

Mitosis

All living things are composed of cells. Some very tiny creatures consist of only one cell, and some don't even have a nucleus. But most plants and animals consist of millions of cells. Even though a plant or animal may have millions of cells, it still begins with only one cell. So how does one cell become a whole plant or animal? This happens through an amazing process called mitosis. Mitosis is cell division that results in two identical cells.

As you just learned, the nucleus of a cell controls everything that goes on in that cell. The nucleus can do this because is contains a vast amount of information. This information is stored in special molecules called DNA. All of the information needed to "build" the particular organism is found in the DNA. Inside the nucleus, the DNA is divided into several long strands called chromosomes.

When a cell is ready to divide, the cell makes a complete copy of each chromosome. When this is done, complete mitosis begins. Mitosis takes place in four major phases. During prophase the wall around the nucleus breaks down and the chromosomes are duplicated. In the second phase, called metaphase, the chromosomes line up in the center of the cell. In the next phase, the duplicates of each chromosome are pulled apart and one set of chromosomes ends up at each side of the cell. This is called anaphase. The final phase is telophase. During telophase a new envelope develops around each set of chromosomes forming two nuclei. Also, in a process called cytokinesis, the cell membrane pinches together to form two new cells. In plant cells, a new cell wall also forms down the center of the cell to divide the cytoplasm. This results in two new cells, often called daughter cells, which are both identical to the original cell.

Through mitosis, plants and animals develop and grow and replace old worn out cells. The most amazing thing of all is that these identical cells somehow know to develop into different kinds of cells after division occurs.

Nearly every cell in a plant or animal experiences mitosis. The only exception is reproductive cells. Egg and sperm cells in animals, and ovules and pollen cells in plants experience a different kind of cell division call meiosis, which produces cells with only one set of chromosomes instead of two.

If you have access to a microscope you may be able to see cells that are experiencing mitosis.

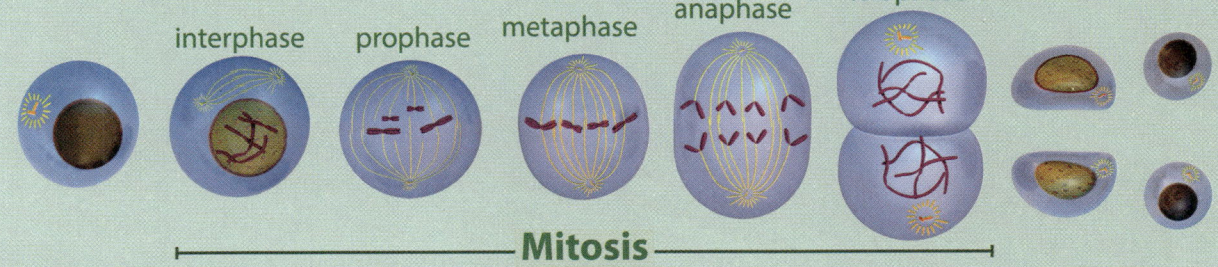

interphase   prophase   metaphase   anaphase   telophase

Mitosis

Purpose: To examine cell division

Materials: microscope, slide, onion, sharp knife, blue food coloring or iodine solution

Procedure:

1. Cut a very thin slice of onion and place it on a slide. Add a drop of blue food coloring or iodine solution to make the parts easier to see.

2. Observe it under a microscope. You should be able to see individual cells that look somewhat like rectangles.

Inside each cell you should be able to see a dark spot which is the nucleus. You may be able to see some cells that have chromosomes lined up in the center or that are being pulled apart. These are cells that are undergoing mitosis.

3. Whether you have a microscope or not, search the Internet and you will find many web sites that show actual cell division or animations of cell division to give you a better understanding of the process.

Cells

Who discovered cells and when? Since most cells cannot be seen with the naked eye, it took the invention of the microscope for them to be seen. The inventor of the microscope was Anton Van Leeuwenhoek from Holland; he was the first person to see microorganisms. However, the first person to record seeing cells was Robert Hooke of Britain, who improved on Anton's microscope by making a compound microscope, one with two lenses, and adding an illumination system. This happened around 1665.

Hooke used this new microscope, one of the best of its day, to study organisms. When he studied the box-like cells of cork, it reminded him of the cells of a monastery. Therefore, he called them cells and the name stuck. So, if you discover something new, choose its name wisely. It just might stick.

Robert Hooke was perhaps one of the greatest experimental scientists of his day. He was largely educated by his father. He was a homeschooler. Among his inventions are the universal joint, iris diaphragm, anchor escapement, and balance spring, which made more accurate clocks possible. He also improved or invented some of the meteorological (weather) instruments of that time. He was a man of many talents.

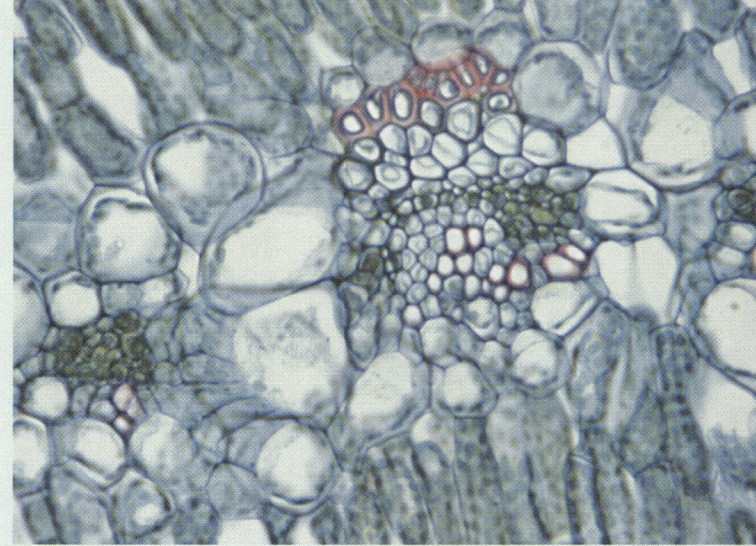

Some facts about cells:

- Cells are the smallest living things known.
- It would take around 10,000 human cells to cover the head of a pin.
- Egg yolks are cells.
- One of the largest cells is the ostrich egg yolk.
- Nerve cells can be up to 3 feet (1 m) long.
- All living organisms are made up of one or more cells.
- All cells come from other cells. They do not just appear.

UNIT 2

Flowering Plants & Seeds

◊   **Describe** the function of each of the organs of flowering plants.

◊   **Describe** why grasses are important to mankind.

◊   **Distinguish** between deciduous and evergreen trees.

◊   **Distinguish** between monocots and dicots.

5

Flowering Plants

God's gift of life to the world

What are the parts of a flowering plant?

Words to know:

roots

stems

leaves

flowers

God created plants on the third day of creation. Genesis 1:12 says, "And the earth brought forth grass, the herb that yields seed according to its kind, and the tree that yields fruit, whose seed is in itself according to its kind. And God saw that it was good." Most plants that we are familiar with are flowering plants. These plants reproduce by seeds that are formed in their flowers. Plants have four distinct organs that do specialized tasks. Can you name them?

The four plant organs are:

- **Roots**—anchor the plant to the soil, absorb water and minerals, and store food.

- **Stems**—hold up the plant's leaves and flowers, transport water and nutrients throughout the plant, and store food. Trees, shrubs, and some vines have stiff woody stems. Flowers, grasses, and other vines have soft flexible stems.

- **Leaves**—manufacture food. Photosynthesis takes place mostly in the leaves.

- **Flowers**—perform reproduction by producing fruits and seeds. Flowers may not always look like you expect them to!

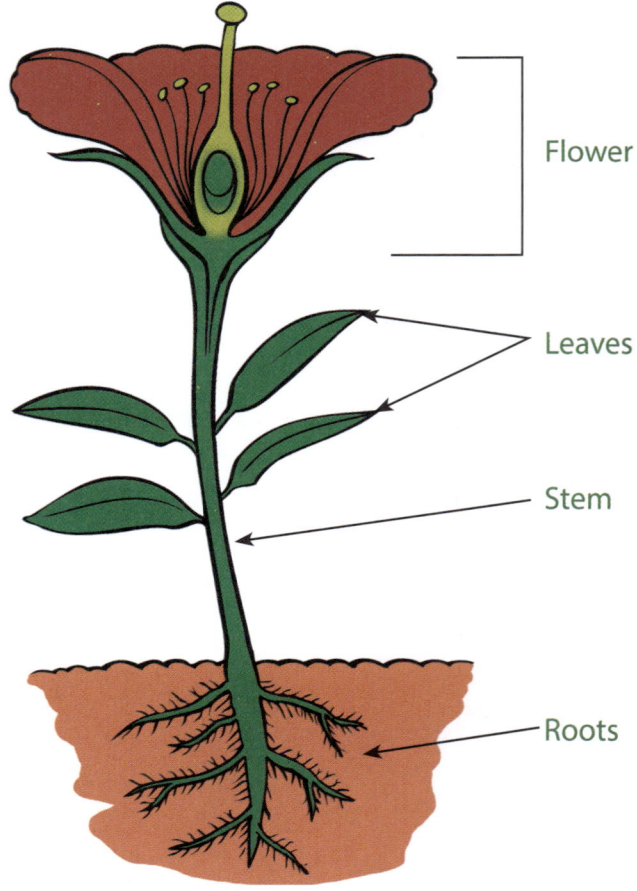

Flower

Leaves

Stem

Roots

Even though almost all plants have these structures, each type of plant is unique. God designed plants with a vast array of sizes, shapes, colors, and purposes. Many plants are easily distinguishable. Even the smallest child knows the difference between a tree and grass, or a rose and a corn stalk. One of the easiest ways to identify plants is by examining their flowers. Each type of plant has a unique flower. Examining these flowers can reveal the wonder and the variety of creation.

What did we learn?

- What are the four major parts of a plant?
- What is the purpose for each part?

Taking it further

- What characteristics other than the flowers can be used to help identify a plant?
- What similarities did you notice between the flowers you examined?
- What differences did you see?
- Can you use size to determine what a plant is? Why or why not? (Hint: Is a tiny seedling just as much an oak tree as the giant oak that is 100 years old?)
- Why might you need to identify a plant?

Examining flowers

We are familiar with many flowers, but there are some unusual ones. Grass, when allowed to grow tall enough, will bloom with very tiny flowers. Most weeds will bloom if allowed to grow. Many wild flowers are considered weeds when growing in our yards but are considered beautiful when growing in the mountains or prairies. Dandelions are a great example of this.

Purpose: To describe and identify flowers

Materials: field guide, notebook, flowers

Procedure:

1. Describe some flowers you are familiar with, such as rose, daisy, carnation, or tulip. Discuss what makes each one unique and how you might try to identify a flower you are not familiar with.

2. Examine a field guide for flowers. Look for identification techniques. These should include but not be limited to:
   - General shape of the flower (bell, ray, etc.)
   - Number and arrangement of petals
   - Color
   - Size

3. Go outside and use the field guide to identify as many flowers as possible in your garden, yard, or nearby field. Dried or pressed flowers may also be used, but are harder to match to the pictures and description in a field guide.

Tiger lily

Rose

Daisy

Tulip

Carnation

🏅 Plants in industry

Flowering plants are vitally important. Not only are they the source of food for nearly every food chain on Earth, but they are also used in many other ways as well. Plants are used in many industries. For example, cotton is used in clothing, trees are used in building, and reeds are used to make baskets. Plants are also very important in making medicines. Choose one of these areas, or another where plants are used in industry, and research the use of plants. Make a short presentation to your class or family so they will understand the importance of plants.

Reeds are used to make baskets.

Cotton plants

Grasses

Do I have to cut it again?

What kinds of grasses are there?

Words to know:

turf grass

forage grass

cereal grass

ornamental grass

A very common flowering plant is grass. One third of all land is covered with some type of grass. Grass is a very important food source for many animals as well as for humans. "But humans can't eat grass," you may argue. Well, that is true for the grass you grow in your yard and for many other grasses as well. But several types of grass, including wheat and oats, are very important foods for humans. Grasses are grouped in the following ways:

- **Turf grass**: This is usually short—only a few inches tall. This is the type of grass used in lawns, on golf courses, at parks, etc.

- **Cereal grass**: This type of grass includes the grains such as wheat, barley, rye, oats, corn, and rice. Breads and cereals are a major source of food for all humans, making this the most important group of grasses on Earth.

- **Forage grass**: This is taller than turf grass. These grasses grow wild in prairies and savannahs. They are also grown by farmers. This is a major source of food for grazing animals including wild

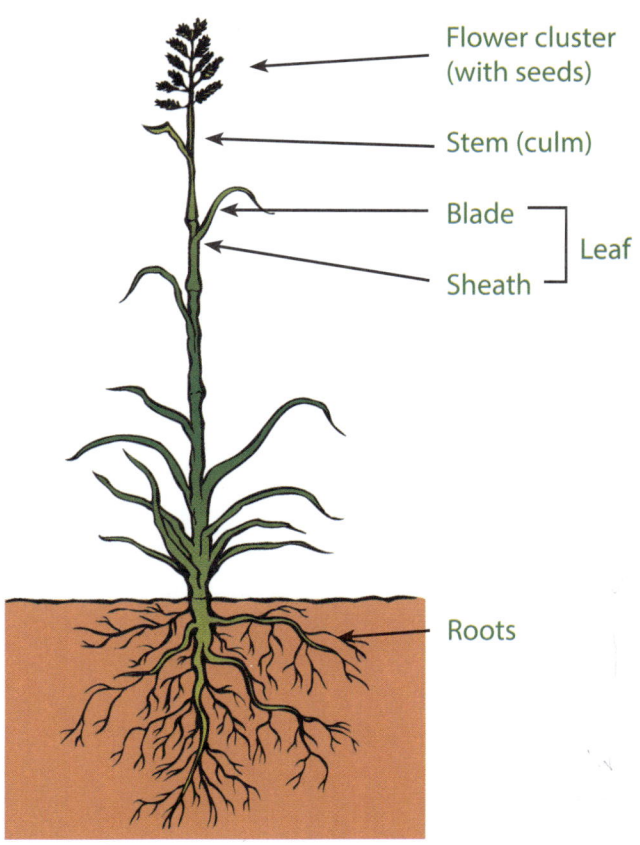

Flower cluster (with seeds)

Stem (culm)

Blade ⎤
     ⎬ Leaf
Sheath ⎦

Roots

animals such as deer and antelope, and domestic animals such as cattle and horses.

- **Ornamental grass**: This type of grass is very tall and usually used in landscaping. Pampas grass is a popular ornamental grass.
- Miscellaneous grass: This type includes sugar cane and bamboo.

🧠 What did we learn?

- Name four types of grass.
- Describe the roots of a grass plant.
- Why are grasses so important?

🚀 Taking it further

- Why can grass be cut over and over and still grow, while a tree that is cut down will die?
- Why is grass so hard to get rid of in a flower garden?
- What part of grass plants do humans eat?
- What part of grass plants do most animals eat?
- Why can a cow eat certain grasses that you can't?

The kernel of the wheat is what is harvested and then ground to make flour.

Examining grass

Purpose: To examine the structure of grass

Materials: grass plant, magnifying glass

Procedure:

1. Carefully uproot a grass plant. Be sure to include as much of the root system as possible, as well as all the foliage growing above ground.

2. Using a magnifying glass, observe the following:

   - Grass has a fibrous root system. It has lots of small roots growing in many directions. Up to 90% of a grass plant's weight is in the roots.

   - The stem is hollow. It grows up through the center of the plant.

   - Leaves grow from the base of the plant. They have a sheath around them. This helps protect the leaves as they grow.

   - If the plant is tall enough, you may observe flower clusters at the top of the stem. These flowers are usually very small and not very noticeable.

   - If the plant has matured enough, seeds could be observed at the top of the stem.

Grass comparison

There are many different kinds of grass used for many different purposes. It is fun to observe and compare different grasses as they grow.

Purpose: To compare grass seeds

Materials: different grass seeds (such as Kentucky blue grass, corn, rye, fescue, wheat, oats), potting soil, baking dish, craft stick, "Grass Comparison" worksheet

Procedure:

1. Obtain as many different kinds of grass seed as you can. You should be able to obtain Kentucky bluegrass seed and corn seeds at any store that sells lawn and garden supplies. Other types of grass seed include rye, fescue, wheat, and oats.

2. Once you have obtained at least two different kinds of grass seeds, observe what each type of seed looks like and record your observations on the "Grass Comparison" worksheet.

3. Next, place two inches of potting soil in a baking dish.

4. Plant several of the first type of seed at one end of the dish. Do not plant the seeds more than ¼ inch deep.

5. Write the type of seed on a craft stick and push the stick into the soil near where you planted the seeds.

6. Plant some of the second kind of seed in another area of the dish and write the type of seed on another craft stick and place it in the soil near where you planted the seeds.

7. Repeat this process for each kind of grass seed that you have.

8. Water the soil each day and record your observations on the worksheet.

9. Continue watering your plants for two weeks. At the end of two weeks, answer the questions on the worksheet.

7

Trees

Did George Washington really chop down a cherry tree?

How are trees classified?

Words to know:

woody plants

herbaceous plants

deciduous

angiosperm

evergreen

conifer

gymnosperm

bark

Challenge words:

crown

growth habit

Plants that grow with a single, tall, woody stem are called trees. These plants need no support and can grow to great heights. Shrubs differ from trees in that they have many stems and low branches. Shrubs generally do not get as tall as trees. Shrubs and trees are both **woody plants**, which means they have stiff stems unlike grasses and many flowering plants that have bendable stems. Those plants are called **herbaceous plants**.

Trees can be grouped into two categories: deciduous and evergreen. **Deciduous** trees lose their leaves in the winter or dry season; **evergreen** trees do not. Trees such as oak, maple, apple, cherry, and dogwood are broad-leaved deciduous trees, but some deciduous trees, like larch and cyprus, have needles. Evergreen trees include pine, spruce, fir, and cedar, but some broad-leaf trees are evergreen, magnolias for example, especially in tropical areas.

Another way to group trees is based on where the seed is found. **Angiosperms** reproduce with flowers, fruits, and seeds. The seeds are in the fruit. The word angiosperm means "covered seed." Most deciduous trees are angiosperms and have broad leaves.

Gymnosperms ("naked seed") have cones instead of flowers. The seeds are not in a fruit. **Conifers**, or coniferous trees, are gymnosperms because instead of flowers, they have cones in which their seeds form. Most coniferous trees are evergreen. Many people may not think that conifer trees have leaves. However, their leaves are often called needles. Ginkgos and cycads are examples of gymnosperms that have broad leaves.

Fun Fact

The tallest known tree in the world is called Hyperion. It is a redwood tree located in a remote part of Redwood National Park, in California. This giant was measured at 379 feet, 4 inches (115.6 meters). That is more than twice as tall as the Statue of Liberty including the base.

A cross-section of a tree trunk showing the growth rings

Trees are different from herbaceous plants because they have a layer of bark as do some vines and most shrubs. **Bark** cells help protect the tree throughout its long life. Trees also have growth rings. As new cells are formed in the region between the bark and the wood, the trunk gets thicker. In cold regions, these cells are produced only during the growing season and not during the winter. Some years the conditions are better for growing than others so the growth rings can vary in size from year to year, and sometimes multiple rings can grow in one year. If a tree is cut down, the rings can be clearly seen inside the trunk (or stem) showing approximately how many years the tree has been growing.

What did we learn?

- What makes a plant a tree?
- How are deciduous and evergreen trees different?
- How are angisperms and gymnosperms different?

Taking it further

- Do evergreen trees have growth rings?
- How long do you think a tree lives?

What kind of tree is this?

Purpose: To learn the difference between deciduous and evergreen trees

Materials: index cards, marker or crayon

Procedure:

1. Label index cards with the following vocabulary words: angiosperm, gymnosperm, broadleaf, needles, flowers, cones, seeds, bark, growth rings, oak, maple, cherry, fir, pine, spruce, and conifer.

2. For each index card, decide if that word applies to deciduous or evergreen trees. Then use a marker or crayon to draw a simple tree (like those shown here) on the back of the card. Some words apply to both kinds of trees, so draw both pictures if appropriate.

Deciduous   Evergreen

3. After completing all cards, sort the cards by the pictures on the back. This will help give an idea of the differences between the two kinds of trees.

🎖 Tree shapes

Although trees are most often identified by their fruit and their leaves, many trees also have a distinctive shape. Most deciduous trees have trunks that do not go all the way to the top of the tree. Instead branches grow up and out from the trunk. These branches form the crown of the tree. Oak trees often have a rounded crown; elm trees usually have a narrow tall crown.

Many evergreen trees on the other hand have trunks that go most of the way up especially conifers. The lower branches tend to grow longer than the upper branches giving most evergreen trees a more triangular shape. The way a tree grows, or the shape its branches form, is called its growth habit. You will learn more about growth habits when you study stem structures in lesson 14.

Purpose: To study the growth habit of trees

Materials: paper, pen or pencil

Procedure:

1. Carefully observe the shape and growth habits of several trees. Try to observe both deciduous and evergreen trees.

2. For each tree, make a detailed drawing of the tree showing its shape and branch structure.

3. Label the drawing with the tree name if you know what kind of tree it is. Use a field guide to help identify the tree.

4. Write a description of its growth habit below your drawing.

5. Make sketches of any flowers, cones, fruit, or seeds you find on the tree.

6. Make a bark rubbing of the tree's bark by placing a blank piece of paper against the trunk and rubbing the paper with a crayon or pencil.

7. Make a leaf rubbing or collect a few needles to glue onto your drawing.

8. Compile all of your drawings and rubbings into a notebook. Save these drawings to include in your final project, which you will do in lesson 20.

Redwoods

The Biggest Living Things on Earth

What do you think of when someone asks you, "What is the biggest living thing on Earth?" Do you think of an elephant or a blue whale? While these are very large mammals, they are not the largest living things on Earth. For that answer we need to look into the woods at the trees themselves. The largest living thing on Earth, the organism with the most mass, is a redwood tree, or sequoia. There are three types of sequoia trees: the Coastal Redwood, the Sierra Redwood, and the Dawn Redwood. The name *sequoia* comes from the Cherokee word for patriarch.

Let's look at a few interesting facts about these truly amazing trees:

1. A redwood's trunk can be from 8 to 20 feet (2.4–6 m) across.

2. Many redwoods grow to be over 300 feet (90 m) tall.

3. One redwood tree was large enough to build 22 five-room houses from its wood.

4. Some redwoods are believed to be over 2,200 years old. That means they were already 200 years old when Jesus came to Earth as a man.

5. The redwood forest has the highest amount of biomass per square foot of any place on Earth. There is as much as 8 times more living material in a redwood forest than in a tropical rainforest.

6. These trees are so tall that they can't pump water to their topmost branches. At the top, the tree absorbs water through its leaves. That is why the tallest redwoods only grow in areas that have a lot of fog.

7. The bark of the redwood can be up to one foot (30 cm) thick.

8. When fire hurts the bark of a redwood it chars

into a heat shield, thus reflecting the heat away from the tree.

9. The tree itself is either distasteful or poisonous to most pests, and the wood resists rot caused by water.

10. The wood was used to make car batteries until the 1960s because it can withstand strong acid.

11. A live redwood that gets knocked over can continue to grow. The limbs pointing upward can turn into new trees.

12. One tree was so large that a road has been put through it.

You can see these amazing trees in northern California's Sequoia National Park.

8

Seeds

Germination—the beginning of life

How do seeds grow into plants?

Words to know:

germinate

dormant

Challenge words:

seed dormancy

embryo dormancy

external dormancy

scarification

seed coat dormancy

stratification

internal dormancy

double dormancy

Seeds have the potential to produce new plants. God designed each plant to "yield seed according to its kind, and the tree that yields fruit, whose seed is in itself according to its kind." (Genesis 1:12) This means that a bean seed grows into a bean plant, a watermelon seed grows into a watermelon plant and so on. You won't get a tomato if you plant an apple seed. When you want to grow a new plant, you usually buy a package of seeds and plant them in your garden. You water the ground, and after a few days you see a plant coming up through the dirt. But, have you ever wondered why those seeds don't begin to grow into new plants while they are in the package?

Seeds must have just the right conditions before they will **germinate**, or begin to grow. What do you think those conditions might be? If you plant a seed in the winter, will it grow right away or does is wait to start growing until the spring time? It waits until spring. Why do you think that is?

Most seeds need three things before they will start to grow: water, oxygen, and warmth. Seeds don't sprout in the package because they are too dry. The seeds remain **dormant**, kind of like being asleep, until they have just the right conditions to germinate. What would happen if a seed germinated without these conditions? The plant that sprouts from the seed would not be likely to survive. Without

Fun Fact

The U.S. Department of Agriculture has a special center called the National Center for Genetic Resources Preservation, whose goal is to conserve genetic resources of crops and animals important to U.S. agriculture and landscapes. Most of the information is stored as seeds. At the main storage facility in Fort Collins, Colorado, there are over 1.5 billion seeds being stored in coolers and freezers. Stored at 0°F (-18°C), many believe the seeds may stay good nearly indefinitely.

water and oxygen the plant cannot perform respiration and break down the food it needs to grow so it would soon die. Without warmth the plant would freeze. A seed that germinates in poor conditions is basically wasted if the plant does not survive. If seeds continued to sprout in poor conditions, it is possible that some plants could become extinct. So God designed seeds to only germinate when the plant is likely to become strong and healthy.

Fun Fact

The oldest mature seed that was germinated into a viable plant was a 2,000-year-old Judean Date Palm seed, recovered from excavations at Herod the Great's palace on Masada in Israel; this seed was germinated in 2005.

What did we learn?

- What conditions must be present for most seeds to sprout or germinate?
- Why do seeds require these three conditions to begin growing?
- Is soil necessary for seeds to germinate?

Taking it further

- If plants don't need soil to germinate, why do plants need soil to grow?
- Our seeds germinated in the dark. Can the plants continue to grow in the dark?
- How long can seeds remain dormant?

Germination

Purpose: To test the hypothesis that a seed needs water, oxygen, and warmth to germinate

Materials: five glass jars (one with airtight lid), paper towels, bean seeds, steel wool, black construction paper, "Germination Data Sheet"

Procedure:

Label the jars 1–5. Jar number 4 needs to have an airtight lid.

Jar 1: This is the control that has all three conditions: water, oxygen, and warmth.

1. Place a couple of moist (not dripping) paper towels loosely in the jar.
2. Place 3 or 4 bean seeds between the side of the jar and the paper towel.
3. Place the jar in a windowsill or other warm place.
4. Keep the paper towels moist for several days.

Jar 2: This jar will have no warmth.

1. Prepare the jar as above but place it in the refrigerator.
2. Keep the paper towels moist.

Jar 3: This jar will have no water.

1. Prepare this jar as above but use dry paper towels.
2. Place it in the window sill with Jar 1.
3. Do not add water to the towels at any time.

Jar 4: This jar will have no oxygen.

1. Prepare this jar the same as jar 1, but place a piece of steel wool inside the top of the jar and seal it with an airtight lid. The steel wool will react with the oxygen in the jar to use it up, leaving no oxygen in the jar.
2. Place this jar with jars 1 and 3.
3. Do not open this jar or add more water.

Jar 5: This jar will have no light but will have water, oxygen, and warmth. This jar is necessary because we introduced an unexpected variable when we placed jar 2 in the refrigerator. Most refrigerators are dark when the door is closed, so we need to make sure that the lack of light is not what is keeping the seeds from germinating in the refrigerator.

1. Prepare jar 5 like jar 1.
2. Make a tube around the jar with black construction paper and tape it so it can slide on and off to check the progress of the seeds. Make a paper lid to set over the top of the tube to block out the light.

Conclusion: Check each jar every day for several days and record what you see on your "Germination Data Sheet." After a few days you should see some of the seeds in jars 1 and 5 begin to sprout, while the beans in the other jars do not. Discuss these observations with your parent or teacher. Save the plants growing in jar 1 for use in later lessons.

🏅 Seed dormancy

Although you have just set up an experiment to demonstrate the conditions under which most seeds will germinate, you should know that not all seeds will germinate under these conditions. Some seeds will remain dormant even when the needed conditions for germination are present until one or more other conditions are met. This is called seed dormancy.

There are two types of seed dormancy. External or seed coat dormancy occurs when the seed coat prevents the oxygen and water from reaching the seed, thus preventing germination. The second type is internal or embryo dormancy. Internal dormancy occurs when the inner tissues of the seed do not respond until certain additional conditions have been met. Both types of dormancy exist to prevent the seed from sprouting before conditions are favorable for the plant to grow. If a seed fell from a plant in the fall and germinated right away because it was still warm and there was oxygen and water available, the new plant might not survive the winter. Therefore, God designed seeds to wait for the right conditions.

Seeds with external dormancy have tough or thick seed coats. Something must happen to the seed coat to break it down or crack it open before the seed will germinate. Breaking the seed coat is called scarification. Scarification generally happens during the winter. Freezing temperatures or bacteria in the soil can break down or crack the seed coat. In other cases, the scarification occurs in the digestive system of an animal that has eaten the seed. Scarification allows the seeds to germinate in the spring when temperatures warm up and water is available.

In agriculture it is sometimes desirable to scarify the seeds so they can be planted without waiting for natural processes to do the job. Commercial growers often soak seeds in sulfuric acid to break down the seed coat. In other instances, seeds are soaked in hot water to soften and break down the seed coat. Seeds that have been scarified are planted right away because they will not store well.

Internal dormancy also prevents seeds from germinating at the wrong time; however, this dormancy is not dependent on the seed coat. Many types of seeds require that the internal moisture drop below a certain level before the seeds can germinate. This allows the seed to dry out during the winter and then be ready to germinate in the spring. Often commercial growers dry seeds quickly and then package them to sell in the spring.

Other seeds with internal dormancy must experience an extended period of cold temperatures or a period of warm moist temperatures followed by a period of cold temperatures before they will germinate. This process is called stratification. Stratification occurs during the winter months, thus the seeds are ready to germinate in the spring. Again, commercial growers often perform stratification of seeds by chilling seeds in refrigerators so they are ready to plant at the appropriate time.

Finally, some seeds have double dormancy. They must be scarified and stratified before they will germinate. The scarification must occur first, followed by the stratification. Through all these processes it is apparent that God designed seeds to be able to survive harsh conditions and to germinate when conditions are favorable to the growth of new plants.

Monocots & Dicots

What's inside that seed?

How many parts does a seed have?

Words to know:

embryo	plumule
seed coat	radicle
cotyledon	endosperm
monocot	hilum
dicot	

Challenge words:

hypogeal	epigeal

Seeds were designed by God to produce new plants. Each seed has an **embryo** or "baby" plant inside of it. It also has a **seed coat** on the outside to protect the seed until conditions are right for germination. The largest part of the seed is the **cotyledon** (cot-el-LEE-dun), which supplies nourishment for the sprouting plant. Upon germination, the cotyledon sometimes becomes the first embryonic leaves of the seedling. Some seeds have just one cotyledon and are called **monocots,** and some have two cotyledons and are called **dicots**. Dicot seeds can easily

be split in half, but monocots cannot. Plants can grow for several days (and sometimes weeks) using the nourishment from the cotyledons. But eventually, the plant must be put into soil to receive nutrients through its roots.

On the inside of the seed are the plumule and the radicle. The **plumule** is the part that grows

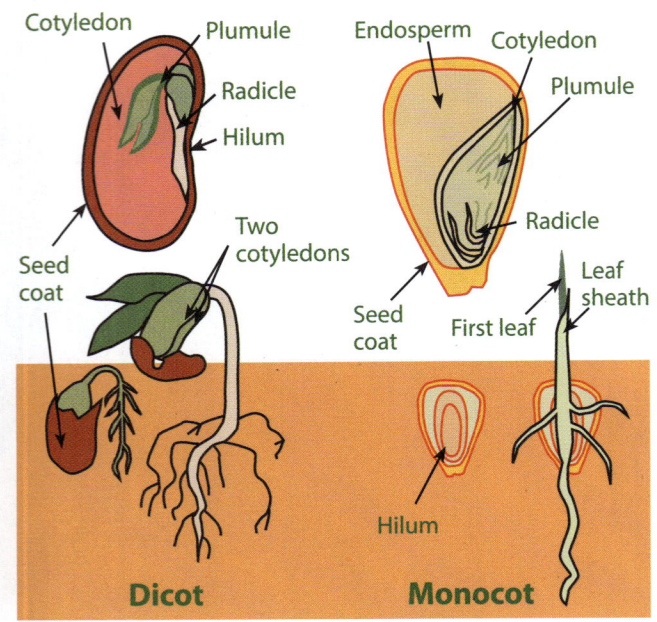

Dicot

Monocot

into the stem and leaves of the plant. The **radicle** develops into the roots. In some seeds, you can also see the **endosperm**. This is an area in the seed made up of mostly starch, which provides nutrients for the newly developing plant. Seeds with an endosperm still have a cotyledon. The cotyledon absorbs energy from the endosperm and transfers it to the developing plant.

On the outside of a seed is a scar called the **hilum** that shows where the seed was attached to the ovary in the flower. This is a little bit like your belly button.

It is amazing that a hard little seed has the potential to become a large plant, able to make more seeds and continue the cycle.

🧪 Seed dissection

Purpose: To dissect seeds and identify their parts

Materials: bean seeds, corn seeds, scalpel or sharp knife, magnifying glass, jar, paper towels

Preparation: Soak several bean and corn seeds in a cup of water overnight.

Dicot—Procedure:

1. Remove several of the bean seeds, which are dicots, from the water in which they have been soaking.

2. Carefully examine the outside of the seeds. You should be able to identify the seed coat and the hilum (see diagram above left).

3. Remove the seed coat from one of the beans. What can you observe about the seed coat? Compare this to the seed coat of a bean that has not been soaked in water. How has the water affected the seed coat?

4. Now, use your fingernail to split the seed open. The two halves of the seed are the cotyledons.

5. Now find and identify the plumule and radicle. Can you see the plant's very first leaves?

Monocot—Procedure:

1. Remove several of the corn seeds, which are monocots, from the water and carefully examine the outside of these seeds. How does the seed coat of the corn differ from the seed coat of the beans?

2. Find the hilum of this seed (see diagram above right).

3. Using a knife, an adult should carefully cut the seed open. Monocot seeds have only one cotyledon. Also, monocots store the food for the embryo in the endosperm surrounding the cotyledon. The cotyledon absorbs nutrients from the endosperm during germination.

4. Identify the plumule and radicle using the diagram.

5. Take several of the corn seeds and "plant" them in a jar or plastic cup using moist paper towels to hold the seeds against the inside of the jar, just as you did with the beans in lesson 8, jar 1.

6. Place this jar with jar 1 so these seeds can germinate. We will continue to use these jars in future lessons. Remember to keep the towels moist but not drippy. If possible, you will want to keep these seeds growing for several weeks to observe the complete life cycle of a plant from seed to flower.

What did we learn?

- What differences did you observe between the monocot and dicot seeds?
- What parts of each seed were you able to identify?
- What is the plumule?
- What is the radicle?
- What is the purpose of the cotyledon?

Taking it further

- Why did you need to soak the seeds before dissecting them?
- What differences do you think you might find in plants that grow from monocot and dicot seeds?

Where do seeds germinate?

As you learned in the last lesson, seeds must have special conditions before they will germinate. They must have water; germinating seeds absorb up to 200% more water than the dormant seed contained. If you have any dry seeds left, compare the size and shape of the dry seeds with the seeds that have soaked in water overnight. You will probably see that the soaked seeds are bigger and less wrinkled.

Seeds also need oxygen. The germinating seeds need oxygen to begin cellular respiration. Recall from lesson 1 that even though plants make their own food, they must also be able to break down that food and turn it into energy. This is cellular respiration and it requires oxygen to react with the sugar in the plant. The food stored in the cotyledon is usually stored in the form of starch, so an enzyme called *diastase* converts the starch into sugar and then the oxygen reacts with the sugar to give the new plant energy to grow.

Once favorable conditions exist, germination generally occurs in one of two ways. **Hypogeal** germination is where the cotyledons stay underground as the plant emerges. Peas experience hypogeal germination. Other plants experience **epigeal** germination. The cotyledons of these seeds come up out of the ground and may appear to be leaves. However, they will have the same shape as the seed and not the normal shape of the leaves of the plant. The first true leaves will grow on the stem above the cotyledons. Observe your bean and corn plants as they grow and determine which plants experience hypogeal germination and which experience epigeal germination.

If you have access to other kinds of seeds, you can dissect them to determine which are monocots and which are dicots. Do you still have some grass seed left from lesson 6? Do they appear to be monocots or dicots? You can also plant other types of seeds and see which ones you are able to get to germinate.

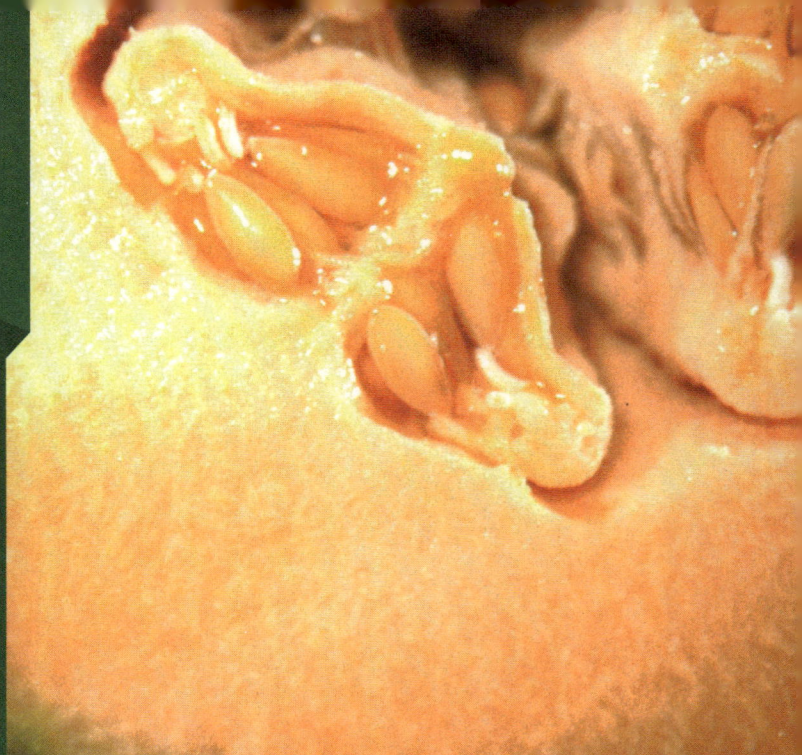

10

Seeds—Where Are They?

They get around.

How are seeds dispersed?

Words to know:

disperse

Challenge words:

seed dispersal   dispersing agent

All flowering plants produce seeds in their flowers, but we don't always see them. Where is grass seed? We often cut our grass before it has a chance to flower. Where are the ornamental flower seeds? We often throw the flower away or cut it back before the seeds are produced. Where are seeds for trees? Some places to look for seeds are in pinecones and in fruits. Seeds can also be found just about anywhere that plants grow naturally. Many times when we consider a plant to be dead, it is actually in its final stages of producing and dispersing its seeds so it can produce new plants in the future. So, look for flowers that have lost their bloom and you will probably find seeds. You often have to look very closely because many seeds are very small, especially seeds for garden or ornamental flowers.

God not only had a plan for plants to produce seeds, but He also had a plan for getting those seeds to new places. What would happen if all of a plant's seeds fell right next to the plant? The plants would quickly get too crowded and not grow well. So God designed plants with special ways to **disperse** or scatter their seeds. What ways can you think of? Many plants have delicious fruit around the seeds so animals will eat the fruit. In many cases, the animals eat the seeds along with the fruit. The fruit is digested but

An apple's seeds are in the core.

A pile of maple seed "helicopters"

the seeds pass through the animal and are deposited in a different location along with its waste. Animals also help disperse seeds when the seeds get caught in their fur, like the burrs that get caught in your socks when you hike in the woods. Later those seeds fall off and are then in a new location.

Seeds can also be dispersed by wind. Many seeds are designed to float on the wind. Have you ever tried to catch dandelion fluff? Those floating white umbrellas are seeds moving to a new location. Maple trees produce seeds that twirl like helicopters and float on the wind as well.

A third method of seed dispersal is the exploding seed pod. Some plants literally shoot their seeds out when they are ready. These seeds may go a few feet from the plant or many miles, depending on the weather conditions. The touch-me-not, vetch, and meadow cranesbill send their seeds out in this manner. Whatever the method for getting seeds spread out, God designed plants so that they continue to make more plants.

What did we learn?

- What are three ways seeds can be moved or dispersed?
- Where are good places to look for seeds?

Taking it further

- How do people aid in the dispersal of seeds?
- What has man done to change or improve seeds or plants?
- If a seed is small, will the mature plant also be small?
- Do the largest plants always have the largest seeds?
- Why do you think God created many large plants to have small seeds?
- Can you name a plant that disperses its seeds by the whole plant blowing around?

Fun Fact

The huge fire that occurred in Yellowstone National Park in 1989 seemed to many to be a disaster. But scientists discovered that many of the pinecones in the forests only open up and disperse their seeds in extreme heat such as during a fire. These seeds grow in the fertile soil left behind by the fire. So we see that God planned a way to grow a new forest to replace the one destroyed by the fire.

Fun Fact

Certain orchids of the tropical rain forest produce the world's smallest seeds. One seed weighs about one 35-millionth of an ounce and some seeds are only about 1/300 of an inch (.085 mm) long. The coco de mer is a spectacular giant palm that grows in the Seychelles in the Indian Ocean. The nut of the coco de mer is the largest seed produced by any plant. It can weigh up to 44 pounds (20 kg).

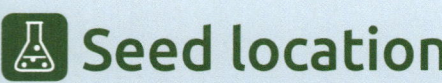

Seed location

Purpose: To see where seeds are found

Materials: several types of fruit, pinecones

Procedure:

1. Gather several types of fruits and open them up and find their seeds.

2. Compare the seeds. Which seeds have softer seed coats? Which are harder? Which seeds appear to be dicots? Which are monocots? Compare their sizes, shapes, colors, etc.

3. Observe several pinecones. Are there any seeds easily seen?

4. Remove several of the scales from one of the cones. Two seeds should be seen at the base of each scale if the pinecone has not already dropped its seeds. As pinecones mature, they become larger, and as the air becomes hotter and dryer, the scales open up, allowing the seeds to drop out.

5. To observe the effects of heat on pinecones, place several pinecones whose scales are tightly shut in a foil-lined baking dish and bake them at 200 degrees Fahrenheit for 30 minutes.

6. Remove the pan from the oven and observe the scales. While the pinecones are baking you can do the next activity: seed dispersal.

Seed dispersal

This activity can probably be done in your yard but if you do not have many plants with seeds around, plan a trip to the park or a nature area to do this activity, or use a book with pictures.

Using the "Seeds Get Around" worksheet, go outside and try to find at least one seed from each category on the worksheet. Draw a picture or glue the seed to the worksheet.

Water dispersal

The movement of seeds away from the parent plant is called seed dispersal. Seed dispersal is very important to prevent the new plants from competing with the parent plants and with each other. What resources would plants be competing for if they are growing near each other? How does seed dispersal show God's plan for plant survival?

We already discussed several ways that seeds are dispersed. When something other than the plant itself helps to disperse the seeds that force is called a **dispersing agent**. Animals and people can be dispersing agents. So can the wind. One important agent not mentioned yet is water. Many plants that grow in or near water have seeds that are dispersed by the movement of the water.

Seeds that fall into a stream or a river can be taken many miles away from the parent plant before they wash up on shore where they can begin growing. Other seeds fall into the ocean and are taken away by the tide. One of the largest seeds in the world, the coconut, is dispersed by water. How can a seed as large as a coconut float in the water to be carried to a new location?

Purpose: To see which seeds are likely to be dispersed by water

Materials: several types of seeds (include a coconut if possible), "Water Dispersal Test" worksheet

Procedure:

1. On the "Water Dispersal Test" worksheet, write the name of each type of seed you are going to test.

2. Write "yes" in the "Will it Float?" column if you think the seed will float. Write "no" if you do not think it will float. This is called making a hypothesis. This should be a good guess based on what you know about things that float and things that sink.

3. Fill a sink with water and gently drop one of each kind of seed into the water.

4. Fill in the chart with the results of your test. Write "yes" if it floated and "no" if it sank.

5. Check your results against your predictions. Were you surprised at your results? Checking your hypothesis is very important. If some of your predictions were wrong, examine the seeds more closely to try to understand why you got an unexpected result.

6. If you have a coconut available, have an adult help you open it up. How is the coconut shaped on the outside? How is it shaped on the inside? The inside of a coconut is hollow. This makes it able to float even though it is much larger and heavier than some other seeds.

"It is not the style of clothes one wears, neither the kind of automobile one drives, nor the amount of money one has in the bank, that counts. These mean nothing. It is simply service that measures success."

—*George Washington Carver*

George Washington Carver was a very rare man. He started off in life with nothing, as a slave. He was born around 1864 on the Moses Carver plantation in Diamond Grove, Missouri. Shortly before he was born, his father died in an accident. While he was still a baby, he and his mother were kidnapped by Confederate night riders (slave raiders); his brother James was left behind. Moses Carver, his owner, found him and paid his ransom after the war, but his mother was never heard of again. Susan and Moses Carver gave George their last name and reared him and his brother as their own children. They must have done a very good job instilling the right values in him when you consider his later life.

When George was young, he was too ill or weak to work in the fields so he spent his time doing household chores and gardening. He also spent long hours exploring the woods, developing a keen interest in plants at an early age. He spent his childhood collecting rocks and plants and earned the nickname, "The Plant Doctor."

At age twelve George left home in order to continue his education in a more formal setting. Since there were no schools in his area that allowed black students to attend, he moved to Newton County in southwest Missouri. Here he worked as a farmhand and studied in a one-room schoolhouse. He later went to Minneapolis, Kansas, for high school.

In 1890 George enrolled at Simpson College to study painting and piano, in which he excelled. His teacher was Etta Budd, whose father was a professor at Iowa State College. She helped him find work with different families around Indianola. As his art teacher and friend, she wanted to help him.

Miss Budd saw that George had a real talent with plants. She told him he would never be able to support a family working as a painter. And she offered to go with him to Iowa State to study science. After he thought about it, he decided to go.

Etta discovered that at Iowa State, George was not allowed to eat with the other students, but instead had to eat his meals in the kitchen because he was black. Etta found this situation to be unacceptable. She brought him into the dining hall where the white students ate. There she ate with him until the students in the school accepted him.

Carver was a brilliant student and excelled in biology. Upon graduation he was offered a teaching position. Carver was not only the first black student at Iowa State College of Agriculture and

Mechanic Arts (today, Iowa State University), but he was also the first black person hired as a teacher there.

A few years later, Booker T. Washington convinced Carver to move south to work at Tuskegee Normal and Industrial Institute for Negroes as the Director of Agriculture. Carver worked there until his death in 1943.

Carver had a strong desire to help the people of the South. Growing cotton depletes the soil, so Carver sought ways to help the southern farmers become profitable after the Civil War. He devised a crop-rotation plan with soil-enriching plants such as peanuts, peas, soybeans, sweet potatoes, and pecans. Carver convinced the farmers to use his rotation method to rebuild the soil. The problem was that there was little demand for peanuts and soybeans.

So Carver invented 300 uses for peanuts and hundreds more for soybeans, pecans, and sweet potatoes. Some of his inventions utilizing these crops included adhesives, axle grease, bleach, buttermilk, chili sauce, fuel briquettes, ink, instant coffee, linoleum, mayonnaise, meat tenderizer, metal polish, paper, plastic, pavement, shaving cream, shoe polish, synthetic rubber, talcum powder, and wood stain.

Of the hundreds of inventions he came up with, Carver only patented three. The rest he gave away to benefit mankind. It is easy to see why he was considered a great man. When asked about charging for his inventions, he would respond with, "God gave them to me. How can I sell them to someone else?" In 1940 he donated his life savings to establish the Carver Research Foundation at Tuskegee, for continuing research in agriculture.

Carver was a very remarkable man. He was once offered a position with a salary of over $100,000 per year. (That is about the same as a million dollars per year today.) He turned the offer down so he could continue his research on behalf of his countrymen and the South.

"He could have added fortune to fame, but caring for neither, he found happiness and honor in being helpful to the world."

– Epitaph on the grave of
George Washington Carver.

UNIT 3

Roots & Stems

◊ **Explain** the types and functions of roots.

◊ **Explain** the types and functions of stems.

◊ **Describe** the growth of plant stems.

11

Roots

A great foundation

How do roots help a plant?

Words to know:

vascular tissue   fibrous root

root cap   taproot

Challenge words:

primary root growth   Zone of elongation

secondary root growth   Zone of differentiation

zone of cell division   Root hair

You may recall from our lesson on cells that many cells working together form a tissue, and that many tissues working together form an organ. Plants have four main organs: roots, stems, leaves, and flowers. Each organ plays an important role.

Do you recall what roots do for the plant? Roots provide the foundation for plants. They help anchor the plant to the ground and keep it from blowing away or falling over. Roots also provide necessary nourishment and water for the rest of the plant. Fine root hairs absorb water and minerals from the soil. Then **vascular tissues**, similar to blood vessels in an animal, carry the water and minerals up to the stem. The vascular tissue also brings food back down from the leaves. The storage tissues in the roots store extra food for the plant.

Root growth occurs at the tip of the root. The **root cap**, at the very end of the root, helps protect the root tip as it pushes its way through the soil.

Plants generally have one of two basic types of root systems. Some plants, such as grasses, have a **fibrous root** system in which the roots spread out in many different directions. They appear to have a lot of little roots and no central root. Plants with fibrous roots generally grow from monocot seeds. Dicots usually produce plants that have a taproot system. **Taproots** have one large central root growing down with many smaller side roots growing outward. Taproots can go deep into the ground. They help plants get water in very dry areas.

Fun Fact

When you look at a plant, think about what is going on below the surface of the soil. There is generally as much of the plant underground as there is above the ground. Think about that the next time you see a tree that is 60 feet (18 m) tall!

Fibrous roots

Taproot

What did we learn?

- What are the four organs of a plant?
- What are the jobs that the roots perform?
- How can you tell what kind of root system a plant has?

Fun Fact

The deepest observed living root, at least 195 feet (59.4 m) below the ground surface, was observed during the excavation of an open-pit mine in Arizona.

🚀 Taking it further

- What kind of plants might you want to plant on a hillside? Why?
- Why are the roots of plants like carrots and beets good to eat?
- Why would a plant with a tap root be more likely to survive in an area with little rainfall than a plant with fibrous roots?

⚗️ Root observation

Can you name some common edible roots? Possible ideas would be carrots, turnips, beets, sugar beets, and radishes.

Purpose: To examine root structures

Materials: carrot, magnifying glass, paper towels

Procedure:

1. Examine an unpeeled carrot with a magnifying glass.

2. Carefully slice one carrot lengthwise. Identify the vascular tissue, storage tissue, root hairs, root tip, and if possible the root cap.

3. Use the magnifying glass to examine the root structures that are visible in the jars of beans and corn that you have been growing since lessons 8 and 9.

Questions:

- Do carrots have a fibrous root or taproot system?
- Are carrot seeds more likely to be monocots or dicots? With the exception of grasses, the majority of the plants we are familiar with are dicots.
- How are the roots of the beans and corn similar and how are they different?
- Were any corn or bean seeds planted "upside down." Are the roots growing upside down?

Root growth

Root growth is very important to any plant. There are two ways that a root grows. First it grows longer. This is called primary root growth. Second, it gets fatter. This is called secondary root growth.

Primary root growth happens in two ways. First, the cells at the tip of the root perform cell division. This creates new cells which push the root deeper into the soil. The region where cells are actively dividing is called zone of cell division, located under the root cap. The part of the root just above the zone of cell division is the zone of elongation. Here the cells themselves become longer, also adding to the length of the root.

Secondary root growth occurs as new cells are produced around the central core. These new cells add to the diameter of the root, causing it to become fatter. Secondary root growth occurs in the area above the zone of elongation, which is called the zone of differentiation (or *zone of maturation*). In this region cells arrange themselves to form the tubes needed to make vascular tissue for transporting the water and nutrients that are absorbed from the ground.

Root hairs form on the outside of the zone of differentiation. Root hairs are tube-like projections responsible for absorbing nearly all of the water and nutrients needed by the plant. Root hairs are very small, usually less than a centimeter long, and very narrow, yet they greatly increase the root's surface area. A plant may have as many as 250,000 root hairs per square inch of root surface. This provides a huge surface area for absorbing water.

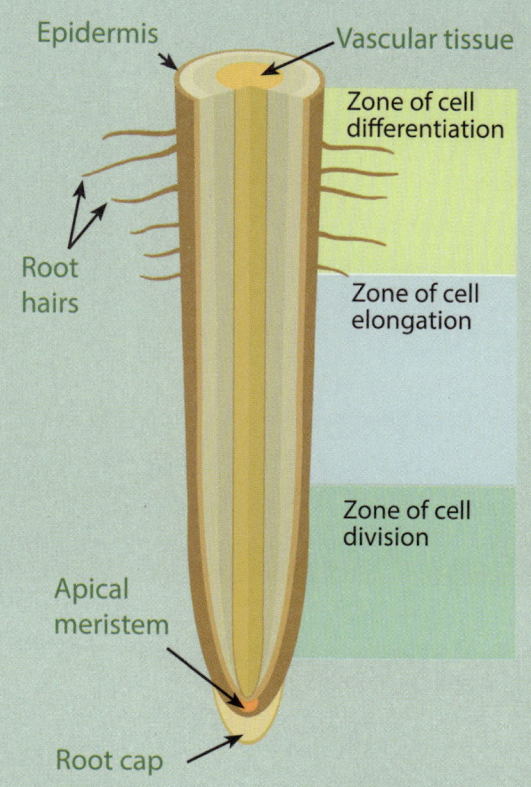

Roots are specially designed for moving through the soil. Not only do the cells add to the length of the root, but the root cap secretes a slimy substance that makes it easier for the root to move between the particles of soil. In addition, because the cells in the root tip are very active, they produce a relatively large amount of carbon dioxide. This combines with water in the soil to produce carbonic acid, which helps to loosen up the particles of soil around the root tip, making it even easier for the root to grow.

Purpose: To observe root hairs on the tip of a root

Materials: radish seeds, magnifying glass

Procedure:

1. Fold a paper towel into quarters.

2. Place several radish seeds between the folds and moisten the paper towel.

3. Place the towel in a warm area and keep the towel moist for several days.

4. When the seeds have sprouted, carefully remove one and use a magnifying glass to observe the root hairs.

12

Special Roots

Not always underground

What are some special kinds of roots?

Words to know:

adventitious roots	prop roots
aerial roots	parasitic roots
pneumatophores	haustoria

Challenge words:

epiphyte

In the previous lesson you learned that plant roots grow in one of two different configurations –fibrous roots or tap roots. This is true for the vast majority of plants. However, some plants have roots growing in unusual places or in unusual ways. These unusual roots are called **adventitious** (ad-ven-TIH-shuhs) **roots**. Adventitious roots can take on many different forms.

Have you ever planted a tulip bulb or looked closely at an onion? You might think that the bulb itself is a root with root hairs growing out of the bottom. However, the bulb is actually a special type of stem and the roots grow individually out of the disc at the bottom of the stem. This is an unusual way for roots to grow so they are classified as adventitious.

Aerial roots, roots that grow in the air instead of in the ground, are another type of adventitious root. There are actually several different kinds of aerial roots and they each serve a different function. In places like the tropical rain forest where there are many large trees, it is difficult for most plants to survive on the ground because the trees block the light from reaching the forest floor. So some plants actually grow on the sides of the trees, up higher where they can receive sunlight. However, this means their roots cannot reach the ground. These plants have special roots that can absorb moisture directly from the air.

Other plants have roots that provide support as they grow up the sides of trees, buildings, and other structures. Ivy plants and many other plants have roots that curl around trellises, fences, and other structures. In addition, some orchids have roots that have chlorophyll, allowing them to perform photosynthesis.

Cypress knees are pneumatophores.

Mangrove trees have prop roots.

Mistletoe is a common parasitic plant.

Another type of aerial root is call a **pneumatophore** (new-MAT-o-for). Pneumatophores are roots that do not grow down, but actually grow straight out or even grow up from the sides of a plant. Most plants that have pneumatophores grow in locations where the plants cannot get enough oxygen from the soil, often because the soil is frequently flooded. So these special roots absorb oxygen from the air. One plant that produces pneumatophores is the mangrove tree. Mangroves grow in very wet soil that is often covered with water.

Prop roots are another type of aerial root. Prop roots grow from the sides of the stem or even from the branches down into the ground. They provide extra support for the plant when the soil is loose or marshy and regular roots are not sufficient to hold the plant in place. Mangroves also grow prop roots to help anchor them to the soil.

Finally some plants have **parasitic roots**. Parasitic roots are ones that grow near the roots of another plant then send out special shoots called **haustoria** (haw-STOHR-ee-uh), which tap into the adjacent plant's roots and "steal" nutrients from the other plant. This is often harmful to the other plant. Mistletoe has parasitic roots.

What did we learn?

- What are adventitious roots?
- What are aerial roots?
- What are prop roots?

Taking it further

- Why do you think that some plants have specialized roots?
- Why do some plants need prop roots?

Root poster

Make a poster explaining all of the different roots you have learned about. Collect pictures of different kinds of roots or draw your own, then use the pictures to make a poster.

Be sure to explain the purpose or function of each kind of root. You should include taproots and fibrous roots on your poster, as well as the roots covered in this lesson.

 # Banyan trees

The banyan tree is a type of fig tree. It starts life as an epiphyte, which is a plant that grows on another plant just for support. Often a banyan tree seed is deposited on a branch or trunk of a tree by a bird that has eaten the figs of a banyan tree. Once this seed germinates, it sends out roots that begin growing downward toward the ground. As the banyan tree gets larger, it sends out more aerial roots that fuse together and often cover the host tree. If the roots grow closely enough they can eventually kill the host. Thus the banyan tree is often called the strangler fig.

The banyan continues to send out prop roots from its branches and can spread out using these roots. So over time, a banyan tree can become very large. Older trees have been known to grow up to 650 feet (200 m) in diameter and 100 feet (30 m) tall.

Banyan trees are native to India but can be found in most of southern Asia and on many tropical islands. They have large leathery leaves and produce a type of rubber as well as a sticky, milky sap. The banyan tree has many uses. First, it is often used as a meeting place because it provides a large shady area. Its sap is used in gardening, to make a polish for copper and bronze, as well as for a medical treatment for skin inflammation and bruising. The roots are often used to make rope, and the bark can be used to make paper. Banyan trees are also very interesting to look at. So if you get a chance, enjoy a rest under the shade of one of these amazing trees.

Fun Fact

Legend has it that Alexander the Great once camped under a banyan tree that was so large it provided shelter for his entire army of 7,000 men.

13

Stems

Connecting it all together

How does the stem help the plant?

Words to know:

xylem	tendril
phloem	thorn
tuber	stolon
bulb	runner

Challenge words:

diffusion	capillarity
osmosis	transpiration

The second organ of the plant that we will study is the stem. Do you recall the functions of the stem? The stem provides support for the plant, serves as a transportation network, and sometimes acts as a storage facility. The stem connects the roots with the leaves and flowers of the plant. It includes the main stem as well as any branches that the plant may have. Woody plants such as trees often have bark on the outside of their stems. Woody plants have stems that get thicker each year and are usually stiff. Woody plants generally come back year after year without dying down to the ground in the wintertime. Herbaceous plants have flexible stems. Some herbaceous plants grow year after year. But many herbaceous plants complete their life cycles in one growing season and then die.

In addition to supporting the plant, the stem's main function is to transport water and nutrients from the roots to the leaves and to transport food from the leaves to the roots. The stem accomplishes this by a series of tubes. The tubes that take water and minerals up the plant are called **xylem** (ZI-lum). Tubes that take the food from the leaves to the rest of the plant are called **phloem** (FLO-em).

grab onto trellises, fences, buildings, and nearly anything else around, including other plants. Rose bushes have special stems called **thorns** that help protect the plant from animals. Strawberries have special stems called **stolons**, or **runners**, which allow them to spread easily over an area and produce new plants.

Some stems also store food for the plant. People often think that potatoes are roots. But they are actually special stems called **tubers** that store extra food for the plant. **Bulbs** such as onions are also special stems that store food. Because this part of the stem is underground, we may think of it as a root, but it is really a stem.

Many plants have other special stems as well. Grape vines, and many other vines, in addition to regular stems, have special stems called **tendrils** that

What did we learn?

- What are the main functions of a stem?
- What do we call the stem of a tree?

Taking it further

- If a tree branch is 3 feet above the ground on a certain day, how far up will the branch be 10 years later?
- What are some stems that are good to eat?

What goes up?

Purpose: To examine the transport system of plants

Materials: food coloring, stalk of celery, bean and corn plants

Procedure:

1. Add a few drops of food coloring to a glass of water until the water is a dark color.

2. Cut off the bottom ½ inch of a stalk of celery to open the xylem and phloem.

3. Place the cut end of the celery in the glass of colored water.

4. After an hour or two you should be able to observe the colored water moving up the stalk of celery. After several hours the color will become visible in the leaves of the celery. You are observing the xylem tubes in action, which are transporting the water up the plant to the leaves.

5. Next, observe the bean and corn plants that have been growing since lessons 8 and 9. What do their stems look like? How are they similar? How are they different?

6. Carefully take two or three of the bean plants and transplant them into a cup of potting soil.

7. Do the same for two or three corn plants. These plants are getting too big to survive much longer on the food stored in the cotyledons of the seed and will need to get nourishment from the soil. Remember to keep the soil moist.

8. If you wish, you can continue growing the rest of the bean and corn plants in the cups without soil and compare their progress with those that you transplanted into the soil.

Water movement in plants

Gravity is constantly pulling down on everything on Earth. It pulls down on you and me and it pulls down on plants. So, if gravity is constantly pulling down on everything, how does water move up the stem of a plant? There are at least three different processes involved in moving the water and nutrients up the plant.

The first process is a special type of diffusion called osmosis. **Diffusion** occurs when molecules move from an area of higher concentration to an area of lower concentration. **Osmosis** is the diffusion of water across a membrane. In plants, osmosis occurs as water molecules pass through the cell membrane of the cells in the root hairs. Because the concentration of water inside the cell is less than the concentration of water outside, water passes through the cell membrane into the cell. Then because the cells inside the root have a lower concentration of water than the root hair cells, the water moves into the inner cells. This lowers the concentration of water in the outer cells allowing more water to move into them.

Inside the xylem, another force called capillarity helps to move the water upward. **Capillarity** is the attraction that the water molecules have for each other and the walls of the xylem tubes. Water molecules have a slight attraction to each other due to their molecular structure. This attraction helps to draw the water up the stem. You can observe capillarity by placing the edge of a paper towel in a dish of water. Even though only the edge of the paper towel is in the dish, water will quickly move up the towel.

Capillarity can raise water only a few feet, so another force must exist to draw the water farther up the plant. **Transpiration** is the evaporation of water from the plant into the atmosphere. When water evaporates from the leaves, it lowers the water pressure; this allows water from below to flow upward into the leaf. All three processes—osmosis, capillarity, and transpiration—work together to move liquids up the stem of a plant.

Roots & Stems

Stem Structure

How they are put together

How is a branch structured?

Words to know:

shoot

terminal bud

axillary bud

lateral bud

node

internode

Challenge words:

excurrent branching

deliquescent branching

A stem is the major part of a plant that you see above ground. It provides the main shape and structure of the plant. Trees have a single large stem (trunk) with many smaller stems branching off of the main stem. Bushes have lots of smaller stems growing directly out of the ground. These stems also branch out, but are generally much smaller than tree branches. Flowers and garden plants also have stems and many of them branch out as well. Stems may look very different from one plant to another, but they serve the same purposes. The stem's main purpose is to transport nutrients and food throughout the plant.

A **shoot** is a new stem that grows from the seed or off of the main stem. As the shoot grows, it forms buds. The **terminal bud** is the bud at the end of the stem. This is where most of the stem's growth occurs.

Other buds form along the stem. These buds are called **axillary buds**, or **lateral buds**. Lateral buds grow into flowers or new shoots that form new branches. If a plant grows aerial roots they will start from a lateral bud. Leaves also grow from lateral buds.

The point where a leaf grows on a stem is called a **node**. Most leaves grow from the sides of the stem or from the end of the stem. However, in many grasses the leaves grow from the bottom of the stem. The area of the stem between two nodes is called the **internode**. The diagram shows the major structures of a stem. 🌿

Terminal bud   Lateral buds   Node   Internode

What did we learn?

- What are the major structures of a stem?
- Where does new growth occur on a stem?
- What gives the plant its size and shape?

 ## Taking it further

- What will happen to a plant if its terminal buds are removed?
- How are stems different between trees and bushes?

- In your experience, do flower stems have the same structures, including terminal buds, nodes, etc., as bush and tree stems?

Examining stems

If possible, examine a bush or tree that has new growth. Try to identify each part of the stem. Look for terminal and lateral buds, new shoots, nodes, and internodes.

After examining the plant, draw a picture of the stem. Be sure to identify all the parts that you observed.

Branching

Just like roots, stems also have primary growth (growing in length) and secondary growth (growing in diameter). Primary growth occurs at the tips of the branches at the terminal buds and the lateral buds. In the spring, meristematic cells in the buds begin to divide causing the buds to lengthen. As the terminal bud grows it also produces hormones which control the growth in the lateral buds. Most plants produce more lateral buds than they need. Some of the lateral buds receive the hormone to make them grow and others remain dormant. However, if some of the growing buds are damaged the remaining buds can be stimulated to grow in their place. This is God's back up plan to ensure that the plant grows well even if a hailstorm damages the plant or an animal eats some of the buds. If the extra lateral buds are not needed they eventually fall off.

As you learned in lesson 7, different plants have different growth habits. This is because some plants have strong growth in the terminal buds and other plants have strong growth in the lateral buds. Plants that have strong growth in the terminal buds have a more vertical growth habit. These plants are said to have **excurrent branching**. Trees such as pines, firs, and redwoods have this type of growth.

Plants that have strong growth in the lateral buds have a more horizontal growth habit. This type of growth is called **deliquescent branching**. Oaks and willows, and most other deciduous trees, have this type of growth.

Secondary growth occurs in stems as the cells inside the stem divide and grow. This causes the stem

Oak trees exhibit deliquescent branching.

Fir trees exhibit excurrent branching.

to become larger in diameter. Secondary growth occurs primarily in trees and shrubs. You will learn more about secondary growth in the following lessons.

Look at the growth habit for the plants that you just examined. Is the growth primarily vertical or horizontal? Can you easily see a trunk or primary stem most of the way up the plant? Then the plant has excurrent branching. If you see lots of branches dividing over and over, the plant has deliquescent branching. Which plants in your yard have excurrent branching and which have deliquescent branching?

Stem Growth

Further up and further out

Why do trees have rings?

Words to know:

epidermis

cuticle

cambium cells

heartwood

sapwood

Challenge words:

vascular bundles

The stems of all plants grow longer and branch out to some extent. In young plants, the outer layer of the stem is called the **epidermis**. This is the same name given to your skin. And just as your skin helps protect your body, the epidermis of the stem protects the plant. The very top layer of the epidermis is called the **cuticle** and contains a waxy substance that prevents the plant from losing or absorbing too much water. In herbaceous plants, those that only live one year, or those that die down to the ground each winter, young flexible stems are the only type of stem that we see. However, in woody plants that continue to grow larger each year, like trees and shrubs, the stems grow outward as well as lengthwise.

Inside the epidermis are special cells called **cambium cells**. These are thin-walled cells located around the xylem and phloem cells. As the stems become more mature, they develop more xylem and phloem cells. The cambium cells also expand and push outward on the epidermis. The epidermis cells begin to harden and die. These dead cells eventually become bark. After several years of growth, the bark can become very thick on some trees. The bark on other trees remains relatively thin, depending on the type of tree. Because bark cells are dead, they cannot grow and stretch as the tree trunk enlarges. Therefore, the bark often cracks or peels as the trees become more mature. Still, the bark serves the purpose of protecting the tree from drying out and from disease.

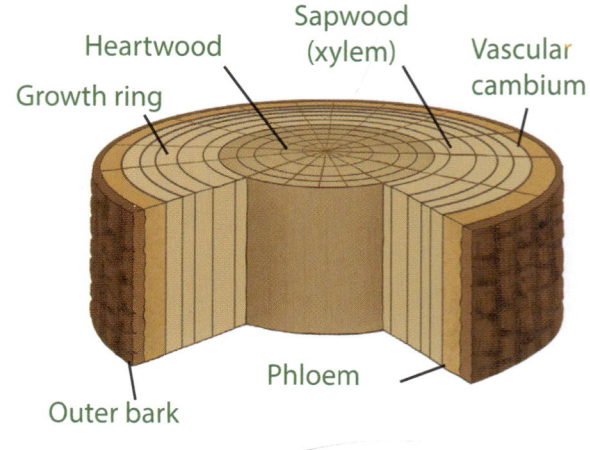

Heartwood

Sapwood (xylem)

Vascular cambium

Growth ring

Phloem

Outer bark

The growth in the cambium, xylem, and phloem cells only occurs during the spring and summer. The cells produced during the spring are a lighter color and bigger than those produced during the summer in temperate regions. As you learned in lesson 7, this produces different colored bands inside the tree, with one band of light- and dark-colored cells for each growing season. In very wet years, there may be multiple rings in a single year.

If a tree lives long enough, eventually the xylem cells near the center of the tree are no longer able to transport fluids. These cells continue to provide support for the tree, but water and other materials no longer flow through the center of the tree. The wood in the center of the tree becomes very hard and is called **heartwood**. The xylem and phloem that are farther from the center of the tree still transport the needed nutrients. The wood in this part of the stem is called **sapwood**, which contains the xylem. The living phloem cells are part of the inner bark.

What did we learn?

- What are epidermis cells?
- What is bark?
- Name three types of cells inside a stem.

Taking it further

- Can we tell a tree's age from the rings inside the trunk? Why or why not?
- If you wanted to make a very strong wooden spoon, which part of the tree would you use?
- Why don't herbaceous plants have bark?

Looking at tree rings

Below is a cross section of a tree trunk. Notice the different colored bands. Each set of light and dark bands represents one year of growth. During years where there is plenty

of water and favorable conditions, the tree produces a larger number of new cells than in years that do not have as much water or that are too hot or too cold. See how many rings you can count and try to figure out how old the tree is. Some rings, particularly the outer rings, are difficult to distinguish so everyone will probably get a different number. Do you notice any rings that are significantly wider or narrower than the rest? What can you guess about the growing conditions during those years?

Scientists have developed a way to take a very thin sample of wood from the inside of a living tree to see the number of rings. This does not harm the tree, but allows the scientist to calculate the tree's age.

Vascular tissue

Woody plants and herbaceous plants all have xylem, phloem, and cambium cells; however, this vascular tissue is arranged differently inside the different types of stems. As you just learned, the vascular tissues are arranged in rings inside a woody stem. Just inside the bark is a ring of phloem tissue. This tissue carries the food down from the leaves of the tree or shrub. Because the phloem is close to the outside of the tree, we are able to drill into a maple tree in the spring and get sap to make maple syrup.

Inside the ring of phloem tubes is a ring of vascular cambium cells. These cells are the ones that divide to form new phloem and xylem cells. Inside the cambium ring is a ring of xylem tissue. The xylem transports water and other materials up from the roots to the rest of the plant. As more xylem and phloem cells are produced, the trunk gets bigger around. As you just learned, if you look at a cross-section of a tree, you see the rings of xylem that have been formed each year. The ring of phloem near the outside of the tree is not as obvious, but is vital to the health of the tree.

Herbaceous stems do not have the same ring structure that woody stems have. The xylem and phloem are found in groups called **vascular bundles**. In dicot stems there is a ring of cambium cells and the bundles are arranged around this ring. Each bundle contains both xylem and phloem tissue with the xylem tissue toward the center of the stem and the phloem tissue toward the outside of the stem within each bundle. This structure is similar to the structure for a young tree or shrub, but the vascular tissue

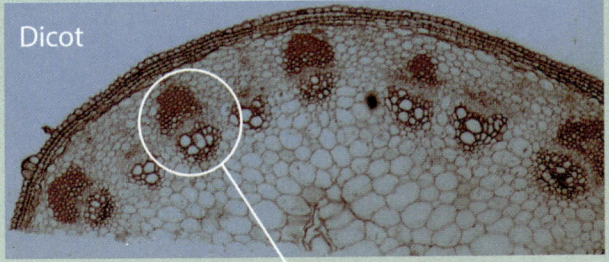

Dicot

Vascular bundle

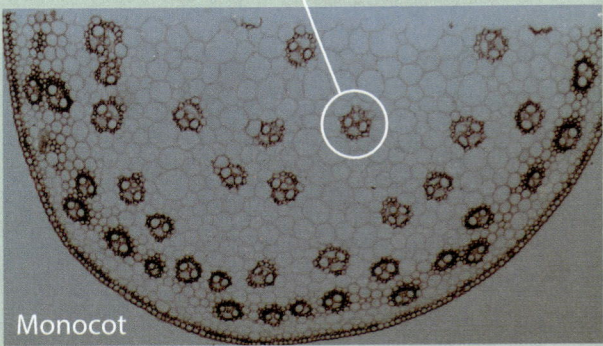

Monocot

does not develop into full rings because the stems only grow for one growing season. In herbaceous monocots, the vascular bundles are more evenly distributed throughout the stem rather than in a circular pattern. Also, some monocots do not contain cambium cells.

In lesson 13, you watched fluids moving up the stem of a stalk of celery. Do you remember how the xylem were arranged in the celery? They were arranged in a circular pattern. Would that indicate that celery is a monocot or a dicot?

Roots & Stems

UNIT 4

Leaves

◊ **Describe** how plants perform photosynthesis.

◊ **Describe** the different shapes and arrangements of leaves.

◊ **Explain** why leaves change colors in the fall.

◊ **Use** a field guide to identify plants.

Photosynthesis

Making food for the world

How do plants make their own food?

Words to know:

photosynthesis

chlorophyll

stomata

catalyst

guard cells

Challenge words:

glucose

starch

sucrose

Leaves are the power plants of the world. They provide food for every living thing on land and thus demonstrate God's love and provision for everything on Earth. You may argue that many animals do not eat plants but only eat other animals and that humans get energy from meat as well as from plants. But keep in mind that the animals that are being eaten got their energy from the plants that they ate and are passing that energy on to the people or animals that are eating them. Thus, all energy ultimately comes from the plants that are eaten. The plants produce this food through an amazing process called **photosynthesis**. Photosynthesis comes from two Greek words that mean "light" and "putting together." Plants use light's energy to combine simple compounds to make sugar for food energy.

Fun Fact

It is estimated that the plants and algae of the world produce 300 billion tons of sugar and starch each year. About 75% of that food is produced in the sea by algae.

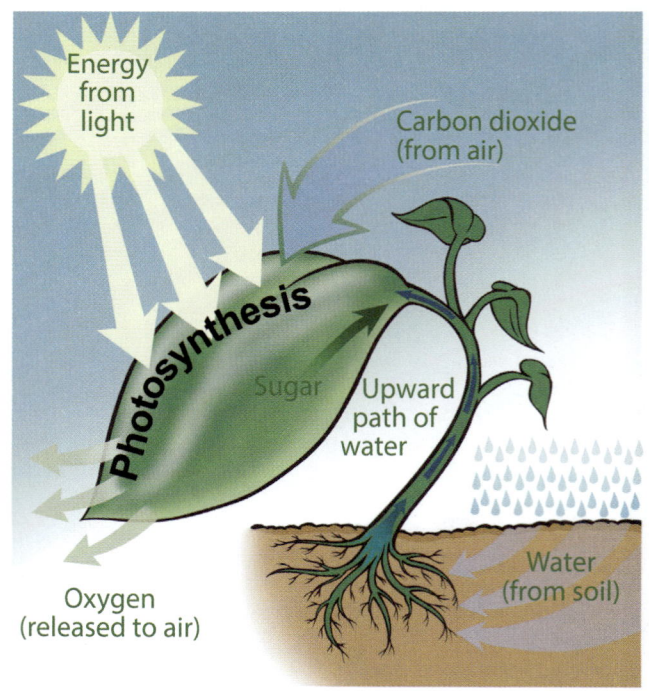

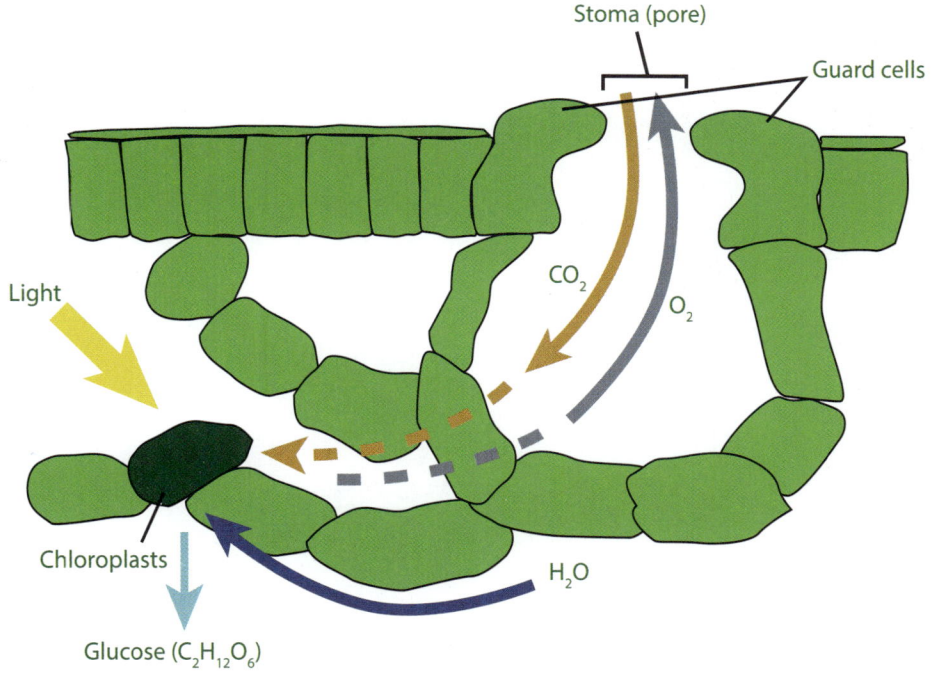

Stoma (pore)

Guard cells

Light

CO_2

O_2

Chloroplasts

H_2O

Glucose ($C_2H_{12}O_6$)

Photosynthesis is a truly amazing process. The roots send water up to the leaves through the stem. The leaves absorb carbon dioxide from the air through **stomata** (singular *stoma*), which are tiny holes in the underside of the leaf. **Guard cells** on each side of the stomata open and close them to allow carbon dioxide to enter or oxygen to exit the leaf. Then, the chloroplasts in the leaves use the energy from sunlight to break apart the water molecules. These molecules combine with the carbon dioxide to make sugar (glucose) and oxygen. The sugar is then changed to starch or fat and stored in the vacuoles of the cells, while the oxygen is released into the air. The food in the vacuoles is then stored in fruit, seeds, stems, roots, and leaves, where it is used by the plant for growth or eaten by animals and humans.

The chloroplasts in the plant cells contain a green pigment called **chlorophyll**. This is what makes leaves and stems green and what makes photosynthesis possible. Chlorophyll is a **catalyst**, which is a substance that causes a chemical reaction to take place very quickly but is not used up in the process. The rate that plants make food through photosynthesis is affected by many factors. If water and carbon dioxide are not readily available, the plant cannot make food quickly. Also, if the temperature is below 65°F (18°C) or above 85°F (30°C), the process slows down. Finally, if sunlight is not available photosynthesis cannot occur.

Perhaps the most amazing thing about photosynthesis is that its waste product—oxygen—is one of the most essential elements for sustaining life on Earth. Plants use carbon dioxide to produce oxygen for people and animals to breath, and the people and animals use that oxygen to break down the food they eat which produces more carbon dioxide for the plants to use in photosynthesis. When we talked about respiration in lesson 1, we mentioned that all organisms use energy to perform the functions of life. Even plants need to use oxygen to change the sugars they make into energy through cellular respiration. But they use less oxygen than they produce, making all of the extra oxygen available for animals to breathe. In a sense, photosynthesis and cellular respiration are opposite processes that complement one another in amazing ways to allow life to prosper. God created a perfect recycling system to keep our air clean and provide food for all His creatures, including us. 🧬

🧠 What did we learn?

- What are the "ingredients" needed for photosynthesis?

- What are the "products" of photosynthesis?

- How did God specifically design plants to be a source of food?

- How does carbon dioxide enter a leaf?

🚀 Taking it further

- On which day of creation did God create plants?

- On which day did He create the sun?

- In our experiment, we found that the plant that got less sunlight grew more slowly than the one that had full sunlight. Is this true for all plants?

⚗️ Sunlight & photosynthesis

Purpose: To test the effects of sunlight on photosynthesis

Materials: three fast-growing potted plants, two cardboard boxes, scissors or knife, "Photosynthesis Data Sheet"

Procedure:

1. Label 3 fast-growing plants (mint plants are a good choice) with the letters A, B, and C.

2. Place all three plants in the windowsill or other sunny area.

3. Measure the height of each plant and record it on the "Photosynthesis Data Sheet."

4. Cut several holes about the size of a half dollar into a cardboard box. About half of the total area of the box should be cut away.

5. Place this box over plant B.

6. Do not cut any holes in the other box and place it over plant C. Plant A should not have a box over it.

7. Each day, for the next several days, remove the boxes and pour the same amount, approximately ¼ cup of water, on the soil of each plant.

8. Measure the height of each plant and record that on your data sheet.

9. Make observations about the plants and the soil and record these on your data sheet as well. As soon as you are done making observations, replace the boxes.

Conclusion: After several days, you should begin to see significant differences in the growth of the three plants. By limiting the amount of sunlight available to two of the plants, you are reducing their ability to perform photosynthesis and therefore their ability to grow. At the end of the experiment, write your conclusions on the bottom of the data sheet summarizing what you learned from this experiment.

🏅 The photosynthesis reaction

Photosynthesis occurs when chloroplasts break apart water and carbon dioxide molecules in the presence of sunlight, and then recombine those atoms to form sugar and oxygen. This is a very simplistic explanation of photosynthesis. Let's take a closer look at what is really happening. The molecules that are coming into the leaves are carbon dioxide and water. A molecule of carbon dioxide contains one carbon atom and two oxygen atoms, CO_2. You probably already know that water, H_2O, contains two hydrogen atoms and one oxygen atom. These molecules are broken apart and the atoms are used to build sugar and oxygen molecules.

The type of sugar that is formed as a result of photosynthesis is called **glucose**. Glucose production takes place in two phases, called the light-dependent reactions and the light-independent reactions. One molecule of glucose contains six carbon atoms, twelve hydrogen atoms, and six oxygen atoms, $C_6H_{12}O_6$. Oxygen atoms are more stable in pairs, so the oxygen atoms that are not used to build the glucose molecule combine together in pairs to form O_2. Obviously you can't build a glucose molecule from just one carbon dioxide and one water molecule. You must actually have six of each of these molecules to build just one glucose molecule. When you use six carbon dioxide molecules and six water molecules to build one glucose molecule, you have twelve oxygen atoms left over which combine to form six O_2 molecules. We have taken a lot of words to explain this process, but scientists prefer to use symbols to explain how this works. The scientific explanation looks very much like a mathematical equation (see below).

Once photosynthesis is complete, the plant now has glucose that can be used for energy. However, it is more efficient to transport and store larger molecules than the relatively small glucose molecules so glucose molecules are linked together to form **sucrose**, which is a larger sugar molecule, or **starch**, which is a long chain of glucose molecules linked together. These larger molecules are stored in fruit, leaves, stems, and roots for later use by the plants that made them and for use by the animals and people that eat them.

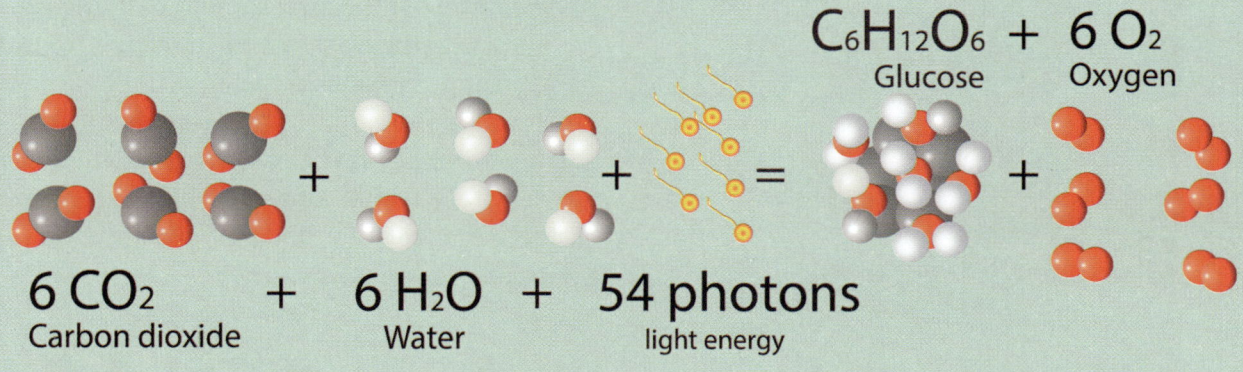

$$C_6H_{12}O_6 + 6\,O_2$$
Glucose   Oxygen

$$6\,CO_2 + 6\,H_2O + 54\ \text{photons}$$
Carbon dioxide   Water   light energy

Purpose: To better understand the photosynthesis process

Materials: "Photosynthesis Building Blocks," scissors, tape

Procedure:

1. Make copies of the "Photosynthesis Building Blocks." You will be starting with six carbon dioxide molecules and six water molecules.

2. Cut the molecules into separate atoms.

3. Tape the atoms together to form one glucose molecule and six oxygen molecules. If you have more than one copy of the worksheet, you can make more than one glucose molecule.

4. Tape two glucose molecules together to form sucrose. If you really like to cut and tape, you can make several glucose molecules and tape them together in a chain to form starch.

Leaves

17

Arrangement of Leaves

Maximizing sunlight

How are leaves arranged on a plant?

Words to know:

opposite leaf arrangement

alternate leaves

whorled

rosette

Challenge words:

bract

spine

succulent leaves

We saw in our last lesson how leaves use water, carbon dioxide, and sunlight, with the help of chlorophyll, to make food through a process called photosynthesis. We also found that if a plant does not get enough sunlight it will not be able to make enough food and it grows more slowly. Therefore, it is reasonable to think that plants should have their leaves exposed to as much sunlight as possible. And that is exactly what we see when we examine how leaves grow on different plants. God designed plants so their leaves can have maximum exposure to the sunlight.

Leaves grow in one of four specially designed arrangements on stems. Where the leaf grows from the stem is called a node. How the nodes are arranged and how many leaves grow from each node determines the arrangement of the leaves.

Some plants have two leaves that grow from each node on opposite sides of the stem, then the next set grows on opposite sides of the stem but 90 degrees rotated from the previous set of leaves. These plants are said to have an **opposite leaf arrangement**. Maple trees, coleus, and mint plants all have an opposite arrangement for their leaves.

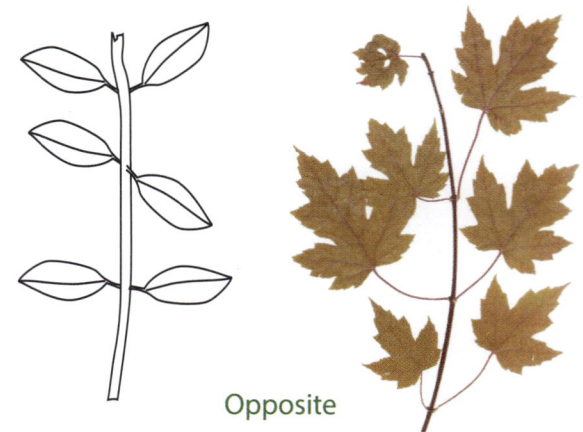

Opposite

Many trees' leaves are arranged in an alternate pattern. Only one leaf grows from each node. A leaf grows on one side of the stem, and then the next leaf grows farther up and on the other side of the stem. Plants with **alternate leaves** include apple, oak, and birch trees.

Alternate

Some plants have three or more leaves that grow from the same node on a stem. This arrangement is called **whorled**. A lily is an example of a plant with a whorled leaf arrangement.

Whorled

The final arrangement of leaves is the **rosette**. All the leaves on these plants grow from the bottom of the stem like petals of a flower. A dandelion is an example of a plant with leaves in a rosette arrangement.

Rosette

In addition to the arrangement of the leaves, God also designed the leaves with the ability to turn toward the sun and follow the movement of the sun, thus further maximizing their exposure to sunlight. This works in a fairly simple manner. When one side of a plant is exposed to a large amount of light, the plant attempts to maximize the amount of photosynthesis it can perform by exposing a larger surface area to the light. The tip of the plants can measure the amount of light coming from each direction. It then sends large concentrations of the plant hormone auxin to the cells of the shady side of the plant. This chemical causes those cells to lengthen, and the whole plant bends towards the light source. Plant leaves usually maintain approximately a 90-degree angle toward the sunlight.

Leaves

🧪 Observing leaf arrangement

Purpose: To illustrate leaf arrangements

Materials: sketch pad or paper, pen or pencil

Procedure:

1. Take your drawing supplies into the yard and observe a tree, bush, or plant of your choice.

2. Determine what leaf arrangement it has, then draw and label a picture of the plant. Be sure to emphasize the leaf arrangement in the drawing.

3. Repeat this exercise for as many plants as you care to examine.

4. Combine your drawings into a book. Make a cover for your book. Then share what you have learned with other people.

🧠 What did we learn?

- What are four common ways leaves can be arranged on a plant?

- Why do you think God created each of these different leaf arrangements?

- Why is it important for sunlight to reach each leaf?

🚀 Taking it further

- How does efficient leaf arrangement show God's provision or care for us?

- What other feature, besides leaf arrangement, aids leaves in obtaining maximum exposure to sunlight?

🏅 Special leaves

Just as there are specialized roots and stems that perform certain functions, there are also specialized leaves that perform special functions. You have already learned that tendrils are special stems that curl around solid objects, but some tendrils are actually specialized leaves that curl around solid objects. Tendrils are very sensitive to touch and respond when they encounter a solid object.

Bracts are another special kind of leaf. Often, bracts are leaves that are brightly colored to attract pollinators to a plant with small flowers. They serve the same role as the petals in most plants. Probably the most popular plant with bracts is the poinsettia. What many people think of as bright red petals, are actually bright red leaves that surround very small flowers.

Plants that grow in very dry areas often have special leaves that help conserve water. A cactus has leaves called spines. These are needle-like leaves that have very little surface area so they do not lose much moisture through evaporation. Other desert plants have succulent leaves. Succulent leaves store water. They often have fewer stomata so water stays inside the leaves. These leaves have a swollen or fleshy appearance. An aloe plant is a popular succulent. If you have access to a plant with succulent leaves, you can cut a leaf open and see the water that is stored in it.

Finally, some leaves are used by plants to trap insects. You will learn more about these special leaves in lesson 26. God has designed leaves to provide food for the world and has designed some leaves for other special purposes as well.

A poinsettia has special red leaves surrounding small flowers.

An aloe plant has succulent leaves.

Cactus spines are special leaves.

Leaves

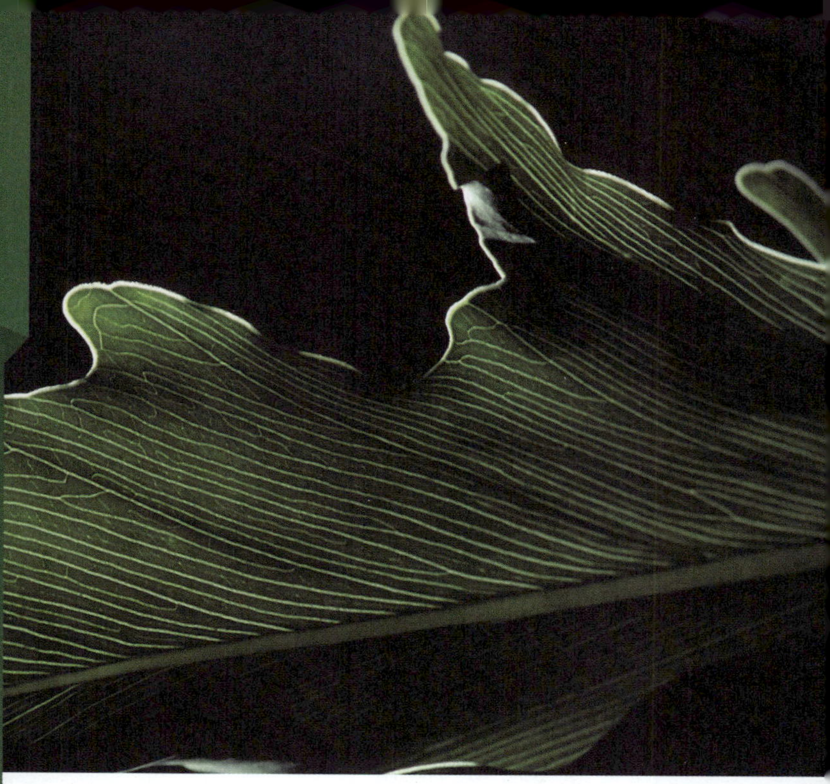

Leaves—Shape & Design

What's your shape?

What patterns do veins make in leaves?

Words to know:

venation

pinnate

palmate

petiole

Challenge words:

leaf margin

entire margin

toothed margin

lobed margin

simple leaves

compound leaves

Most plants around us are broad-leaved plants. Their leaves are wide and relatively flat. There is great variety in the shape of these leaves, so much variety that the shape of a leaf can be used to help identify the plant itself. But there are also many plants that have narrow leaves, needles, or scales.

Grasses have narrow leaves. These leaves are long, thin, and flat. Evergreen or conifer trees have needles. These leaves are hard and thin. They can be as short as ½ inch (1.3 cm) or as long as five inches (12.7 cm). Needles can be flat or square. Their length, shape, and arrangement help us identify the type of

tree they come from. Some evergreen trees such as junipers have flat scale-like leaves.

No matter what the leaves look like, they serve the same purpose—to produce food for the plant. The xylem and phloem from the stems continue into the leaves to bring them water and minerals from

Grasses have narrow leaves, and evergreen tree needles are hard and thin.

Leaves

Pinnate leaves

Palmate leaves

the roots and to carry the food produced by the leaves back to the rest of the plant. The xylem and phloem appear as veins in the leaves. The arrangement of these veins is referred to as **venation**.

Monocots, primarily grasses, have narrow leaves with parallel veins. Dicots, most of the broad-leaved plants, have veins in one of two arrangements. The veins can be pinnate (feather-like) or palmate (hand-like). Leaves with **pinnate** veins have one vein down the center of the leaf with smaller veins branching off to each side. A pinnate arrangement works well for leaves that are longer than they are wide. Nutrients can be taken down the center and out to the edges of the leaf efficiently.

Leaves with **palmate** veins have two or more major veins with smaller veins branching off of these major veins. Wider leaves need more than one major vein in order to efficiently move nutrients throughout the leaf.

God designed these various arrangements of veins to allow for the most efficient transportation of needed materials into the leaf and of food out of the leaf.

 What did we learn?

- What general shape of leaves do monocots and dicots have?
- How can we use leaves to help us identify plants?
- How do nutrients and food get into and out of the leaves?

Taking it further

- Describe how the arrangement of the veins is most efficient for each leaf shape.

Leaves

Observing leaves & veins

Purpose: To observe various leaf shapes and vein arrangements

Materials: sketch pad or paper, pen or pencil, cup, red food coloring, crayons

Procedure:

1. Go into the yard and observe several blades of grass. Be sure to notice the long, thin, flat shape of the leaves. Also note the parallel lines or veins in the leaves.

2. Observe the broad leaves of several trees or bushes.

3. Select a tree or bush with large leaves and carefully remove one or more leaves and take them into the house.

4. Draw a picture of the leaf. Pay close attention to the color and arrangement of the veins. Does the leaf have pinnate or palmate arrangement?

5. Fill a cup with water and add a few drops of red food coloring.

6. Stir the water. Make a diagonal cut across the **petiole** (the "stem" that attaches the leaf to the tree) with a knife or scissors.

7. Put the leaf in the water so the cut end of the leaf can pull up the colored water.

8. Observe the leaf each day for three days and draw a picture of the leaf each day. You should be able to observe the color spreading up the leaf throughout the veins.

9. Another fun idea is to make a leaf rubbing. Place another leaf on a hard surface, lay a piece of paper over it and color back and forth over the leaf with a crayon. This will help bring out the details of the shape of the leaf as well as the arrangement of the veins.

10. Also, observe the leaf shapes and vein arrangements of the bean and corn plants from lessons 8 and 9.

Questions:

- How are the shapes and vein arrangements different?
- Which plant has broad leaves?
- Which has long narrow leaves?
- Which plant is a monocot?
- Which plant is a dicot?

Leaf shapes & margins

One of the most important skills for a good scientist to develop is the skill of careful observation. There is much more to observing leaf shape than just looking at whether the leaves are broad or thin and looking at the venation. First you need to look at the general shape of the leaf. Although every plant has leaves with a shape that is unique to that plant, many plants have leaves with similar shapes. Some leaves are elliptical—they are wide in the center and narrow at the ends. Other leaves are oval with very rounded edges. Some leaves are heart shaped or arrow shaped. Others are ovate or triangular with rounded corners.

Arrow-shaped leaves

Heart-shaped leaves

Entire margin

Toothed margin

Lobed margin

Once you have identified the general shape of the leaf you need to examine the edges of the leaf. The edge of a leaf is called the **leaf margin**. There are three basic types of leaf margins. Leaves with smooth edges are said to have an **entire margin**. Other leaves have jagged edges called a **toothed margin**. Finally, some leaves have very large indentations around the edge and are said to be lobed or to have a **lobed margin**. You learned in the last lesson that leaves are arranged on the stem to allow maximum exposure to the sun. The shape of the leaves also contributes to the amount of sunlight that reaches the other leaves. Lobed leaves allow light to pass through to leaves lower down on the plant.

Finally, you need to determine whether the leaf you are looking at is simple or compound. Most leaves are **simple leaves**, there is one leaf growing from the main leaf stalk or petiole. However, **compound leaves** have several leaflets growing from the petiole. A compound leaf is often confused with a branch with several leaves on it. You can determine if you are looking at several simple leaves or one compound leaf by examining how the leaves are attached. If they all lie flat in the same plane, instead of alternating around the center, then you are looking at a compound leaf instead of several simple leaves. Examine the pictures below and become familiar with the different shapes, margins, and complexities of the leaves so you will be better able to identify the plants they come from.

Simple leaf

Compound leaves

Leaves

Changing Colors

The beauty of autumn

Why do leaves change color in the fall?

Challenge words:

xanthophyll   anthocyanin

carotene

Fall can be the most beautiful time of year. Leaves change from green to bright red, orange, purple, and yellow. Then they fade to brown before falling to the ground. But why do the leaves change color and how do the trees know when to change?

Leaves are green in the spring and summer because of chlorophyll. The other colors are still there but they are drowned out or covered up by the much more abundant chlorophyll. When the length of sunlight each day becomes shorter as winter approaches, the trees seal off the connection between the leaf and the branch. Without new nutrients, no new chlorophyll is formed. As the old chlorophyll deteriorates, the other colors become visible. Eventually, all of the nutrients are used up, the leaf withers, and it falls off.

God designed leaves to fall off so that trees can survive the harsh environment of winter. Trees cannot continue to move liquids around in thin leaves with the temperatures below freezing. Also, the amount of water needed for photosynthesis is often not available in the winter. So many deciduous trees lose their leaves and rest in their growth during the winter. Similarly, evergreen trees rest during the winter. But, because their leaves are not as fragile, they do not lose them each fall.

Leaves

🧠 What did we learn?

- How do trees know when to change color?
- Why do trees drop their leaves?
- Why don't evergreen trees drop their leaves in the winter?

🚀 Taking it further

- Do trees and bushes with leaves that are purple in the summer still have chlorophyll?
- What factors, other than daylight, might affect when a tree's leaves start changing color?

An autumn picture

Purpose: To make a picture of autumn colors

Materials: colored leaves, construction paper, newspaper, heavy book, tag board

Procedure:

1. If it is autumn, collect several different colored leaves. If no leaves are available, cut paper leaves of various shapes and colors from colored construction paper.

2. If the leaves are still pliable, place them between sheets of newspaper and place a heavy book on top of them for several days until they dry out. This will keep them looking good for a longer period of time.

3. Cut out a picture frame from tag board or poster board.

4. Glue the leaves along the edges of the picture frame.

5. Use the frame to demonstrate the beauty that God created all around us, as well as His provision by designing trees to survive the winter.

Leaf pigments

Although most leaves are green, there are four basic pigments that can be found in leaves. Chlorophyll is the most abundant and is what gives leaves their green color. However, other pigments are found in leaves as well. Xanthophyll (ZAN-tho-fill) is a yellow pigment. Many leaves contain xanthophyll as well as chlorophyll. Some leaves look more yellow than green, others look very green, but still contain xanthophyll.

Another pigment that seldom shows through on leaves before fall is carotene. Carotene produces a yellowish-orange pigment. A third pigment found in leaves is anthocyanin (an-tho-SI-a-nin). This pigment produces bright red, blue, and purple colors.

These pigments are not only found in leaves. They are responsible for many of the beautiful colors found in flowers and fruits. Carotene is what makes carrots orange and anthocyanin is responsible for the color of beets and plums.

Purpose: To determine what pigments are present in a plant using paper chromatography

Materials: leaves, coffee filter, coin, fingernail polish remover, dish, tape

Procedure:

1. Gather two or three different leaves. Try to find ones with different colors or different shades of green.

2. Cut a 1-inch wide strip from a coffee filter for each leaf that you collected.

3. Place a leaf over the paper near the bottom of the strip.

4. About 1 inch from the bottom of the paper, roll a quarter or other coin across the leaf, using it to press some of the leaf pigment into the filter paper.

5. Repeat this process for each leaf on its own strip of paper.

6. Before continuing, predict what color of pigments you expect to find in each leaf. Write your predictions on a piece of paper.

7. Pour fingernail polish remover into a small dish to a depth of ½ inch.

8. Place the dish on a counter near the wall and tape each strip of paper to the wall so that it is hanging down with the bottom edge of the strip just touching the polish remover. The polish remover will slowly move up the paper. As it does, it will dissolve the pigments and move them up the paper, too. Different pigments have different weights and will move up a different amount. This will allow you to see the different pigments that are in each leaf.

9. When the polish remover has moved up several inches, remove the strips and place them on a flat surface to dry.

10. Once the strips are dry, compare the pigments found in the various leaves.

Questions:

- Did each leaf have the color of pigments you expected?

- Are you surprised to find so many different colors in them?

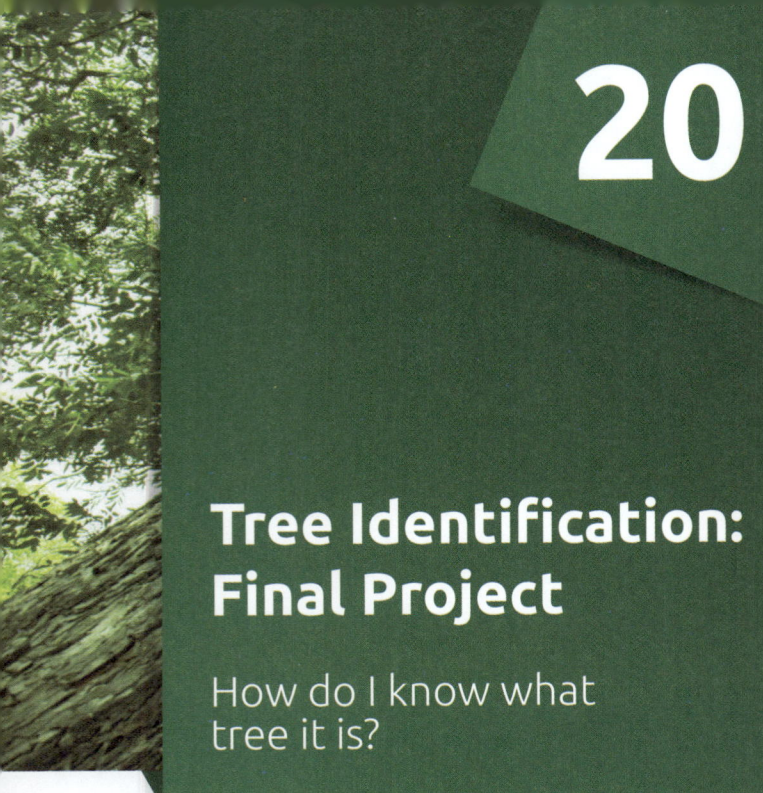

20

Tree Identification: Final Project

How do I know what tree it is?

How many trees can you identify?

Why should you want to learn how to identify trees? You can enjoy trees by looking at them and sitting in their shade. Maybe you'd like to climb into a tree and build a tree house. But to truly enjoy and appreciate the diversity of God's creation, it helps to be able to identify the different plants around us. It is a lot like being a detective as you look for clues.

There are many ways to identify a plant. We use flowers, fruit, and leaves. For mature trees, we can also use the shape of the tree, its bark, and the pattern left on the branches where the leaves were attached. Shape and bark are especially useful for making identification in the winter when leaves and flowers are not available. Leaves are generally available for a longer period of time than flowers and fruit, so they are one of the most useful ways to identify trees or other plants.

To begin with, you need to determine several things about the leaves of the tree. Are they broad leaves, needles, or scales? Are they simple leaves or compound leaves? Compound leaves have several leaflets on each leaf. Look at the arrangement of the leaves. Examine their shape and the arrangement of the veins in the leaves. All of these things give you clues to the tree's identity. Once you have

determined these things, you can use a field guide to help identify the tree. Field guides will give you additional things to look for such as the size of the leaves or the length and arrangement of needles. A good field guide will have pictures of the leaves and often will have pictures of mature trees to aid in identification. If you have access to the Internet, you can get practice identifying trees by their leaves by using an online Dichotomous Tree Key. There's a link to one at the God's Design for Science Online Resource Page at answersingenesis.org/go/godsdesignlinks.

Flowers, fruits, and seeds, including cones and pods, can also be very helpful in identifying a plant.

The shape of the plant can be deceiving if the plant has been pruned excessively. Trees and plants growing in the wild are more likely to have the expected shape than those growing in gardens and parks.

So be a detective, get your field guide, and start practicing. Practice is the best way to learn to tell one plant from another. Eventually, you will be able to identify many plants without the use of a book.

What did we learn?

- What are some ways you can try to identify a plant?

- What are the biggest differences between deciduous and coniferous trees?

Taking it further

- Why do we need to be able to identify trees and other plants?

Final project: leaf notebook

This project will take several days to complete. It will be done in three parts. Part one is to go to an area with a wide variety of trees such as a park or arboretum. There you will collect samples, make observations, and make identifications. Part two is to bring your samples home and prepare them for display. Part three is to prepare a notebook using the information and samples you gathered.

Purpose: To make a tree identification notebook

Part One

Materials: tree field guide, index cards, pencil, zipper bags

Procedure:

1. For each tree, examine the leaves, bark, etc., as described in the lesson. Write all of your observations on an index card. This could include leaf type (needle, broad, scale), size, shape, bark color and texture, leaf arrangement, leaf colors, fruit, flowers, etc.

2. Sketch the general shape of the tree and sketch or describe any other unusual or interesting features you observe.

3. Using the field guide, identify the tree and write the identification on the index card.

4. Carefully remove a leaf from the tree and place the leaf and the index card together in a zipper bag. You can also collect samples of flowers, seeds, pods, cones, etc., and place them in the bag with the leaf.

5. Repeat this procedure for each tree you wish to identify, being sure to place each leaf in a separate bag with its own identification card.

Leaves

Part Two

After you return from collecting leaves, immediately set up a leaf press. This can be as simple as using several heavy books and some newspaper, or you can look on the Internet or in a field guide or other book for examples of building a more elaborate press. The important thing is to press the leaves flat and remove the moisture so they will be able to be displayed without rotting or curling up.

Materials: newspaper, heavy books

Procedure:

1. Spread a layer of newspaper on the counter.

2. Carefully lay several leaves on the paper.

3. Place a number next to each leaf and number the matching index card with the same number.

4. Be sure all the leaves are flat, and then cover them with another layer of newspaper.

5. Place heavy books on top of the newspaper and allow the leaves to sit in the press for several days until they are dry.

Part Three

After the leaves are all pressed and dried, put together a notebook displaying what was learned. Be creative in how you display your leaves and information. Below are just a few suggestions:

- Organize leaves alphabetically, or by type of trees (e.g., pines, oaks, elms, etc.)

- Cut colored paper into rectangles or other shapes to put behind each leaf.

- Type up the information on the index card, or if neatly written, include the card in the display.

- Place the leaves and information on pages of a photo album, or glue to cardstock and place inside plastic protector sheets in a binder.

- Make an index or table of contents as well as a title page.

Keep your eyes open for different varieties of trees. You can always add new samples to your notebook.

Finishing your notebook

You should include the information you gathered on growth habits from lesson 7 in your notebook. Also include any information you can find on each tree that you find interesting. Try to make your notebook something others will enjoy reading.

Leaves

UNIT 5

Flowers & Fruits

◊ **Identify** and **describe** the parts of a flower using models.

◊ **Describe** the purpose of a fruit.

◊ **Explain** different plant life cycles

21

Flowers

The beauty of sight and scent

Flowers & Fruits

What are the parts of a flower?

Words to know:

sepal	ovule
petal	ovary
stamen	fruit
pollen	staminate
pistil	pistillate

Challenge words:

composite flower	disk flower
head	ray flower

The fourth organ of a plant is the flower. (Remember that only angiosperm plants have flowers while gymnosperms produce seeds in structures like cones.) Its purpose is reproduction—it produces the seeds that grow into new plants. There is great variety in flowers: variety in shape, size, fragrance, and color. But nearly all flowers have the same basic parts. Most flowers have sepals, petals, stamens, and pistils.

Sepals are usually green. They protect the flower as it develops by covering the petals until it is ready to bloom. Once the flower blooms, the sepals are usually found at the base of the flower and could be mistaken for small leaves.

Fun Fact

The corpse flower (*Amorphophallus titanum*) is the stinkiest plant on the planet. It grows to an average height of 6½ feet (2 m) and when it blooms it releases an extremely foul odor similar to rotten flesh, which can be smelled half a mile away. It is also known as the *devil's tongue*. This foul-smelling flower was discovered in 1878 in the rainforest of central Sumatra in Western Indonesia.

The **petals** are the most familiar part of a flower. They are the colorful and fragrant part of the flower. Their purpose, besides giving pleasure to those who look at them, is to attract pollinating animals through sight and smell.

The **stamens** are the parts of the flower that produce pollen. **Pollen** is a fine powder necessary for fertilization of the ovules. Stamens are considered the male parts of the flower.

The **pistil** is considered the female part of the flower. It consists of three parts: the lowermost enlarged part called the **ovary**, the style which serves as a conduit between the ovary and the stigma, the uppermost part which recieves the pollen. The ovary produces **ovules**, which are unfertilized seeds or eggs. When combined with pollen, the ovules become seeds.

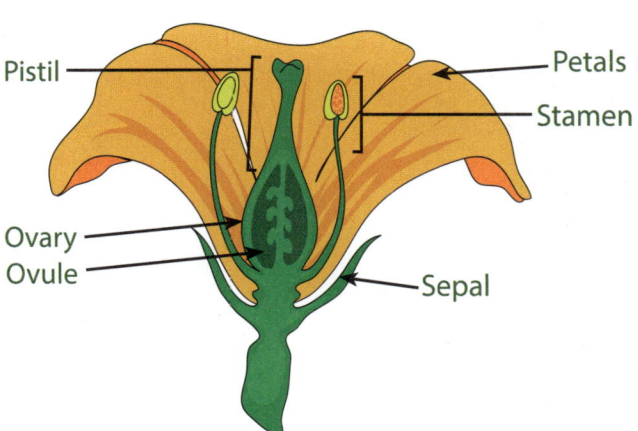

Fun Fact

The orange, brown, and white parasitic plant, *Rafflesia arnoldi*, has the largest flowers. These attach themselves to the cissus vines of the jungles of Southeast Asia. The flower measures up to 3 feet (1 m) across, and weighs up to 24 pounds (11 kg). The rafflesia also smells like rotting meat when it blooms. Although the corpse flower grows taller than the rafflesia, it is technically a collection of smaller flowers so the rafflesia is the largest single bloom.

🧪 Flower model

Purpose: To make a model of a flower

Materials: "Flower Pattern" sheet, scissors, construction paper, hole punch, modeling clay, cornmeal, soda straw, pipe cleaners

Procedure:

1. Cut out each pattern on the "Flower Pattern" sheet.

2. Using the pattern, trace the flower petals on a piece of colorful construction paper.

3. Trace the sepal on a piece of green construction paper.

4. Cut each part out and carefully punch a hole in the center of each piece using a hole punch.

5. Place a 1-inch ball of modeling clay on a piece of construction paper to use as a base for the flower.

6. Place a soda straw, representing the stem, in the clay and press the clay down onto the paper.

7. Put one end of a pipe cleaner through the petal then through the sepal and into the straw, leaving about 1–2 inches sticking out.

8. Cut four 1-inch pieces from a second pipe cleaner.

9. Stick each of these through the petal and sepal into the straw, keeping about ½ inch sticking out. The longer piece represents the pistil and the shorter pieces represent the stamens.

10. Sprinkle a small amount of corn meal on the stamens to represent pollen.

11. You can also cut leaf shapes from the green construction paper using the leaf patterns and tape or glue them to the sides of the straw.

12. Review the purpose of each part of the flower with your parent or teacher.

Fruit is the ripened and often swollen ovary containing the seeds. Using this definition, apples and oranges are fruit, but so are cucumbers, pumpkins, wheat grains, and acorns.

God has designed each of these parts to work together to produce the seed that will grow into another plant.

Most flowers have both stamens and pistils, but some flowers have only one or the other. Flowers with only stamens are called **staminates**, and those with only pistils are called **pistillates**.

 # What did we learn?

- What are the four parts of the flower and what is the purpose or job of each part?

 # Taking it further

- Why do you think God made so many different shapes and colors of flowers?

- If you were to design a flower, what would it look like? Draw a picture of it.

Composite flowers

One of the largest families of flowers is the composite family. You are probably already familiar with many of the flowers in this family. They include the sunflower, daisy, dandelion, marigold, and thistle. So what makes these flowers special? They are called **composite flowers** because what you might consider to be one flower is actually hundreds of tiny flowers on one stalk that together resemble a single flower.

Daisies, sunflowers, and many other composites actually have two different kinds of flowers. The center of the flower is called the **head** and it contains **disk flowers**. These flowers are packed tightly together to form the center of the structure. Around the edge of the head are what appear to be the petals of the flower, but these are actually individual flowers called **ray flowers**. In some composite flowers, only the disk flowers produce seeds, in others both the disk

Thistle

flowers and ray flowers produce seeds.

Some composite flowers only have ray flowers. Dandelions do not have a head with disk flowers. The ray flowers of the dandelion each produce a seed so a single stalk may produce hundreds of dandelion seeds. A few composite flowers only have disk flowers and do not have rays. Thistles are an example of a composite flower with only disk flowers.

Other common composite flowers include asters, dahlias, zinnias, black-eyed Susans, and chrysanthemums. When you see these flowers, closely examine them to see the individual flowers.

Sunflower

22

Pollination

The buzzing bee's job

How does a plant produce seeds?

Words to know:

pollination

self-pollination

cross-pollination

pollinator

nectar

Challenge words:

nectar guide

pollen guide

Pollination **is the uniting of pollen and** ovule to form a seed. Some plants are **self-pollinating**, which means the pollen produced by the flower is used by that same plant to produce a seed. However, most plants need to have pollen from another plant of the same type brought to its flowers in order to produce seeds. This is called **cross-pollination**. But how does pollen get from one plant to another?

Sometimes pollen is transferred by the wind or even the rain, but most of the time an animal such as a bee, wasp, moth, or even a hummingbird transfers pollen. These animals are called **pollinators** and they are attracted to the flowers by color and scent. The petals attract pollinators. Flowers also produce a sweet liquid called **nectar** to attract pollinators.

The animal drinks the nectar of the flower. While moving around, pollen particles stick to the animal's body. Then it flies to another flower for more nectar, where the pollen may fall off. If the pollen lands on the pistil, pollination begins.

The pollen sends a tube down into the pistil until it makes contact with the ovule. This begins the creation of a seed. As the seed matures, the petals fall off, the ovary swells, producing fruit, and finally, when the seeds are mature, they are dispersed.

The yellow pollen grains can be seen on this bee.

Flowers & Fruits

What did we learn?

- What animals can pollinate a flower?
- How can a flower be pollinated without an animal?
- Does pollen have to come from another flower?

Taking it further

- Why do you suppose God designed most plants to need cross-pollination?

 # Pollination flip book

Purpose: To create a book illustrating pollination

Materials: scissors, crayons or colored pencils, stapler, "Flip Book" worksheet

Procedure:

1. Color each page on the "Flip Book" worksheet. Color the flowers identically.
2. Cut the pages apart, put them in order, and then staple the top edges together to form a book.
3. Flip quickly through the pages, and you will see a flower being pollinated to form a seed.
4. After making the flip book, examine your corn and bean plants from lessons 8 and 9. Look for flowers and/or the beginnings of fruit indicating that pollination has taken place. This is the last time we will be examining these plants.

Conclusion:

In your flip book, page 1 shows a bee drinking nectar. You can draw pollen on the bee's body.

Page 2 shows the flower after the bee is gone and shows pollen on the pistil.

Page 3 shows the pollen tube beginning to grow.

Page 4 shows the tube going down into the ovary.

Page 5 shows the tube going down farther.

Page 6 shows the tube going all the way down to the ovule, completing fertilization.

Pollen

Pollination is vital to the survival of plants. Without pollination, new seeds are not formed. But how does the right pollen get from plant to plant? A bee may visit several types of flowers and get more than one kind of pollen on its body. How does the plant know which pollen is right for it? Even though pollen looks like tiny dust to us, the pollen produced by each plant is unique to that plant. The shape and texture of the pollen grains are different for every type of plant. Thus when a bee enters a flower, only the pollen with the right shape and texture will stick to the pistil in that flower. So pollen from a tomato plant cannot pollinate a snap dragon.

Pollen grains from a variety of common plants magnified 500 times

Flowers & Fruits

Getting the bee or other pollinator to visit a flower is very important to that plant's survival. God has designed flowers with many ways to attract pollinators. Some flowers have a sweet scent that attracts bees or moths. We usually like to have these flowers in our homes. Roses and lilacs are two examples of flowers that attract pollinators by scent. Some flowers, such as the corpse flower, produce a smell like rotting flesh. This may not attract very many people, but it is just the right scent to attract flies, which are its main pollinator.

Other flowers attract pollinators by their bright colors. Hummingbirds are especially attracted to the color red which is why hummingbird feeders have red on them. The red petals of many flowers attract hummingbirds for pollination.

Some flowers have patterns on their petals that direct the pollinator to the nectar. They may have stripes or dashes that seem to point to the center of the flower. These patterns are called **nectar guides** or **pollen guides**. Pansies have dark centers and lines that guide the pollinator to the nectar. Some of these guides are not visible to the human eye, but are visible under ultraviolet light. Bees and other insects can see a higher spectrum of light than humans so some flowers have been designed to point the way to the nectar with a pattern that can only be seen by the pollinators.

The shapes of many flowers also contribute to their likelihood of being pollinated. Some flowers are bell shaped which requires the pollinator to crawl inside to reach the nectar and thus increases the possibility of pollination.

Flowers that do not need pollinators, ones that are pollinated by the wind for example, often have small unimpressive petals and no scent; they are not needed. These are often the plants that cause the most problems with allergies because their pollen is easily spread by the wind and thus easily spread to people who are allergic to the pollen. Ragweed is an example of this type of flower. The ragweed flower is very small and has no scent.

You can see the differences in pollen if you examine pollen grains with a magnifying glass or microscope. Obtain one or more samples of pollen and look at them closely with a magnifying glass or microscope. A microscope will best demonstrate the different shapes of the various pollen samples.

Pierre-Joseph Redoute

1759–1840

Pierre-Joseph Redoute is well known for his beautiful drawings and paintings of roses. However, he did more in his life than just draw roses. Redoute was born in 1759 into a family of painters. His father was a painter, as was his grandfather. Pierre-Joseph had little education, but he had a lot of talent. He left home at age 13. Leaving the small country of Luxembourg where he was born, he traveled to Belgium where he hoped to make a living as an interior decorator, doing portraits and commissioned religious works. He loved flowers but was told he could never make a living painting them.

During his travels, Pierre-Joseph become acquainted with other painters and learned from them. Later he joined his older brother in Paris where they painted scenery for the opera. While there, he was brought to the attention of a botanist who asked Pierre-Joseph to paint pictures of plants for his new book. This was something he enjoyed immensely.

After some time in Paris, Redoute was appointed to be the court artist for Queen Marie-Antoinette, and painted the gardens at Petite Trianon. During the French Revolution and the "Reign of Terror" that followed, he was appointed to document the gardens that had become national property.

Later, during the time of Emperor Napoleon, Redoute's career went very well. He produced his most lavish books with plants from around the world. He did his most famous work for the Empress Josephine, Napoleon's first wife. He painted the roses in Josephine's beautiful gardens. This book became his most famous work.

Rosa centifolia foliacea.   *Rosier à cent feuilles, foliacé.*

After the death of Empress Josephine, Redoute was appointed Master of Design for a museum in 1822.

Redoute died in 1840, around the age of 80. The paintings he did of roses, most of which he did in the Empress Josephine's gardens, are still considered some of the best paintings of roses ever done. Although he was told he could never succeed by painting flowers, Redoute continued to follow his dream and became known as the "Rembrandt of Roses" and the "Raphael of Flowers." He gave us some of the most inspiring paintings of flowers that exist.

Flower Dissection

Seeing what's inside

What is the role of each part of a flower?

Words to know:

filament   stigma

anther   style

Challenge words:

receptacle

The best way to appreciate the parts of a flower is to actually observe these parts. By dissecting a flower, you will be able to really visualize the pollination process. As you dissect a flower, you should be able to see not only the major parts that you have already learned about which include the sepal, petals, stamen, and pistil, but you should be

able to see the individual parts that make up the stamen and pistil.

The stamen, which is the male part of the flower, consists of a long stem-like part called a **filament** and a bulge at the top called the **anther**. The anther produces the pollen. The filament supports the anther making it easy for pollinators to bump up against it and collect the pollen to take it to other flowers.

The pistil, which is the female part of the flower,

Flowers & Fruits

Fun Fact

Did you know that when you eat broccoli you are actually eating the flowers of the plant? Broccoli is harvested after the plant produces flower buds but before the buds have a chance to open up.

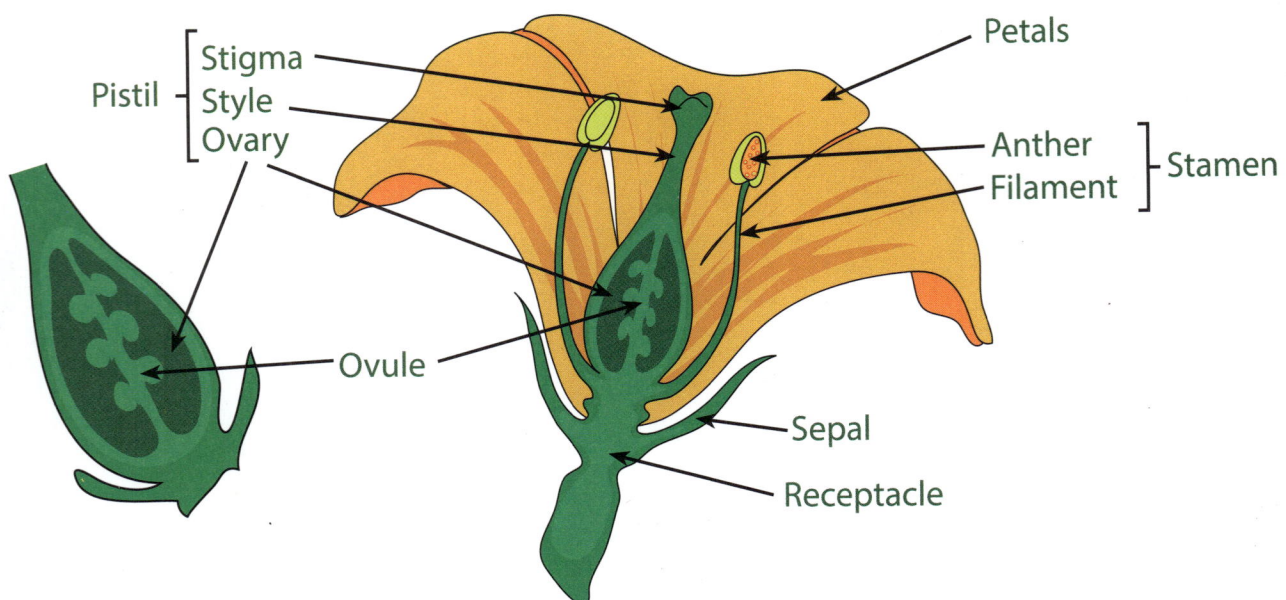

has three main parts. The top of the pistil is called the **stigma**. The stigma is sticky and is the part that receives the pollen when a bee or other pollinator brings pollen into the flower. The stigma is supported by a stem called the **style**. The style is often the tallest part in the center of the flower because it is important for the pollinator to easily bump up against the stigma. At the bottom of the style is the ovary. The ovary contains the ovules, which when pollinated develop into seeds.

🧪 Flower dissection

Purpose: To dissect a flower and examine its parts

Materials: flower (such as lily or alstroemeria), knife or razor blade, tweezers

Procedure:

Examine a flower. Be sure to look carefully for each of the following items.

1. Identify the sepals (usually green and found near the base of the flower). Note, some flowers do not have sepals or lose their sepals after the flower has opened, so your flower may not have sepals

2. Identify the petals. Note their color, scent, and texture. Gently remove the petals and set them aside.

3. Identify the filament and anther of the stamens. The anthers will often have pollen (a sticky yellow substance) on the ends. Gently remove the stamens.

4. Identify the pistil. It should be all that is left of the flower. Most pistils are thin with a bulging area at the bottom. This bulging area is the ovary where the ovules (beginnings of seeds) are. Going up from the ovary you will see the style and at the top you will see the stigma.

5. A parent or teacher should gently cut open the pistil with a sharp knife or razor blade.

6. Locate any ovules. These are generally the size and shape of the flower seed, but are often white or green.

🧪 Optional activity

If you have other flowers available, such as ones growing in your yard, dissect them as well. Some flowers have small parts that may be difficult to identify. Compare how easy or hard it was to identify the parts of the flowers in your yard with the flower chosen for dissection. Compare and contrast the different flowers' reproductive parts.

Review all of the flower parts shown in the diagram, then dissect a real flower and see if you can locate all of these parts.

What did we learn?

- How many ovules did you find?
- What did they look like?
- If possible, compare them to the mature seeds that are ready to be planted.

 Taking it further

- Why are the ovules in the flower green or white when most seeds are brown or black?
- If you planted the ovules, would they grow into a plant?

Composite flower dissection

Purpose: To dissect a composite flower and examine its parts

Materials: composite flower such as a daisy or sunflower, magnifying glass

Procedure:

1. Carefully examine the head and the rays. Look at each type of flower and see how they are similar and how they are different. Examine how the flowers connect to the stem.

2. Carefully remove one of the ray flowers. Use your fingernail to gently open the bottom of the flower. Examine it closely with a magnifying glass. See if you can identify the pistil and stamen.

3. Remove one of the disk flowers. Again gently open the base of the flower and use a magnifying glass to identify the pistil and stamen. These parts are very small and may be difficult to find.

4. Look at how the flowers are connected to the receptacle. The receptacle is the area where the flower connects to the stem. Underneath the receptacle you may find bracts. These special leaves will probably be green and may resemble the sepals on other flowers. The arrangement of bracts is one way that different species of composite flowers are identified.

Questions:

- How do the flowers in the composite flower compare to the flower you previously dissected?
- How are they the same? How are they different?

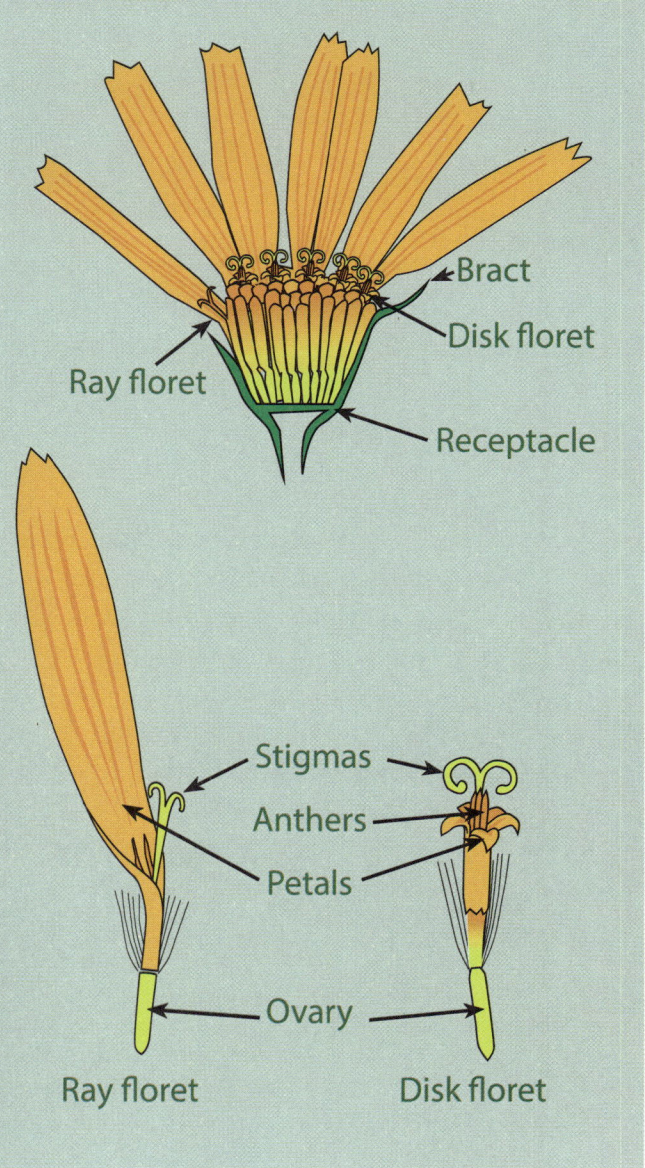

A Rose by Any Other Name Would Smell as Sweet

Roses have been very popular for centuries. In China, the rose has been cultivated for more than 3,000 years. The Chinese had books on the cultivation of roses as far back as 500 BC.

During the Roman Empire, the rose was used for medicinal purposes, as a source of perfume and as confetti in many of their celebrations. The rose was so popular at that time that many Roman nobles made large rose gardens for the public to enjoy. The Romans had a "Festival of Rosalia" on the island of Sicily every year. After the fall of the Roman Empire, interest in roses declined until the Renaissance.

In England during the 1400s, two different colors of roses were used to symbolize two different families who wanted to control England. The Lancasters used the red rose and the Yorks used the white rose. The power struggle between the two families, and most of England, was called "The War of the Roses." King Henry VII ended the struggle by uniting the families in marriage. The new family became known as the Tudors and they were symbolized by the Tudor rose, a white rose edged in red. This is still the symbol of royalty in England today.

During the 1700s the rose was so popular that the royalty of France would use roses and rose water (made by distilling rose petals in water) as a form of money. Napoleon's wife, Josephine, installed a rose garden west of Paris in the 1800s. This is where Pierre-Joseph Redoute did most of his work. Her interest in all exotic plants, and roses in particular, encouraged many people to begin developing different varieties of roses.

In the 1800s the Chinese way of cultivating roses was introduced into Europe. Since that time more than 150 species of roses have been developed. Most of the roses that are sold today can trace their "roots" back to China, thus making roses some of the oldest cultivated flowers on Earth.

24

Fruits

Is it ripe yet?

What kinds of fruit are there?

Words to know:

simple fruit

multiple fruit

aggregate fruit

Challenge words:

succulent fruit	pome
dry fruit	nut
drupe	legume
berry	grain

Once pollination has occurred in a flower and the ovule has been fertilized, the job of the petals is complete so they begin to wither and fall off. But the job of the ovary is just beginning. As the seeds mature, the ovary of the flower swells and ripens. This process is called producing fruit. When you hear the word fruit, what do you think of? Do you think of bananas, peaches, apples, and oranges? These are all fruits. However, any ripened ovary is a fruit from a biological perspective. So a cucumber, walnut, and bean pod are also fruits.

Most fruits are simple fruits. **Simple fruits** form from one flower that has one pistil and one ovary.

Some examples of simple fruits include oranges, grapes, tomatoes, peaches, cherries, and olives. Some simple fruits have only one seed inside and others have multiple seeds from multiple ovules.

But not all plants produce simple fruit. **Aggregate fruit** forms from a flower that has multiple pistils. Some common aggregate fruits are strawberries, blackberries, and raspberries. Each little seed on the outside of a strawberry came from a separate ovary inside a single flower. These separate ovaries combine to produce the single strawberry.

Pineapple flowers each form a fruit that fuse together into a single core.

The third type of fruit we commonly see is called **multiple fruit**. Multiple fruit forms one "piece" of fruit from several flowers. The most common examples of multiple fruit are the pineapple and the fig. In the pineapple, each flower forms a fruit. These fruits fuse together into a single core.

The main purpose of ripened fruit is to disperse the mature seeds so the life cycle of the plant can be complete. Many fruits are attractive to animals. When the animal eats the fruit, the seeds pass through the digestive system and are deposited in another location. Some fruits form into dried seedpods that explode open. Still others form in such a way as to be carried off by the wind. Recall what we learned about seed dispersal. The fruit has completed its job when the mature seeds are dispersed.

Now that you have learned about the four organs of a plant, you should better understand the life cycle of a flowering plant. It begins as a seed. When conditions are right, the seed germinates and the plant begins growing. The leaves perform photosynthesis to make food for the growing plant. As the plant matures it produces flowers that attract pollinators. After pollination, new seeds are formed and dispersed to begin the cycle again. 🌿

What did we learn?

- What is the main purpose of fruit?
- What are the three main groups of fruit?
- Describe how each type of fruit forms.

Taking it further

- What is the fruit of a wheat plant?
- Which category of fruit is most common?
- Why do biologists consider a green pepper to be a fruit?

🧪 Fruit identification

Purpose: To examine the three types of fruit

Materials: apple, strawberry, pineapple, sharp knife

Apple—Procedure:

1. Carefully examine an apple. Look at the outside of the apple, and then carefully slice the apple in half.

2. Observe the outer fleshy layer—the part we like to eat. Then observe the inner papery layer around the seeds. The apple is a simple fruit that develops from a flower with a single pistil. Simple fruits with a fleshy outer layer and a papery inner layer are called pomes.

3. :If you slice an apple across the center, you should be able to see the five chambers of the ovary, each with several ovules that form seeds. The fleshy part outside the core is the receptacle, and the dried sepals can be seen at the bottom where the flower used to be.

Strawberry—Procedure:

1. Carefully examine a strawberry. Each "seed" developed from a separate pistil inside the same flower. This is called an aggregate fruit.

2. Carefully slice the strawberry in half from the top to the bottom. Notice the central core of the fruit. This is formed from the receptacle of the flower.

Pineapple—Procedure:

1. Carefully examine a pineapple. Each diamond-shaped area is a separate fruit. Each fruit formed from a separate flower.

2. Now carefully slice the pineapple in half. Notice the core in the center of the pineapple. This is where each fruit has fused together.

Now cut up your fruit and make a yummy fruit salad.

🏅 Fruit divisions

As you just learned, most fruits are simple fruits. Simple fruits can be divided into two groups. If the fruit has a thick fleshy outer layer it is called a **succulent fruit.** Most of what are commonly called fruits, as well as many "vegetables," are succulents. Other fruits do not have a fleshy outer layer; instead they have a dry cover. These are called **dry fruits**. Each of these groups is further divided into smaller groups.

The succulent fruits are divided into three main groups. If a fruit has a fleshy outer layer with only one hard covered seed in the center it is called a **drupe**. Can you think of any fruits with single hard seeds in the center? Peaches, plums, apricots, cherries, and olives are all drupes. You may not think of an olive as a fruit, but it has the same structures as cherries and other fruits in this category so scientifically it is a drupe.

Succulent fruits with many seeds are called **berries**. When you think of berries you probably think of strawberries and raspberries. These are not berries according to this definition because they are aggregate fruit and not simple fruit. What fruit can you think of that have many seeds inside? Oranges and grapes are berries by this definition. Some vegetables are berries as well. Tomatoes and cucumbers are considered berries.

The third group of succulent fruit is called pomes. A **pome** (pōm) is a fruit that has a papery inner core around the seeds. What fruits can you think of that have a papery core? Apples and pears are pomes.

There are three main groups of dry fruits as well. **Nuts** are dry fruits with hard shells. You are probably familiar with many different nuts. This group includes walnuts, hazelnuts, pecans, and chestnuts. Peanuts do not fit into this group, however, because they do not have a hard outer shell. Instead, peanuts have a pod and so are part of the legume group. **Legumes** are dry fruits that form a pod around the seeds. The third group of dry fruit is the grains. The fruit of the grass family are **grains**. This includes many of the cereal grains and bread grains such as wheat, corn, rye, and oats.

Test how well you understand these definitions by completing the "Fruit Classification" worksheet.

Cherry
Drupe

Tomato
Berry

Apple
Pome

Pecan
Nut

Peanut
Legume

Wheat
Grain

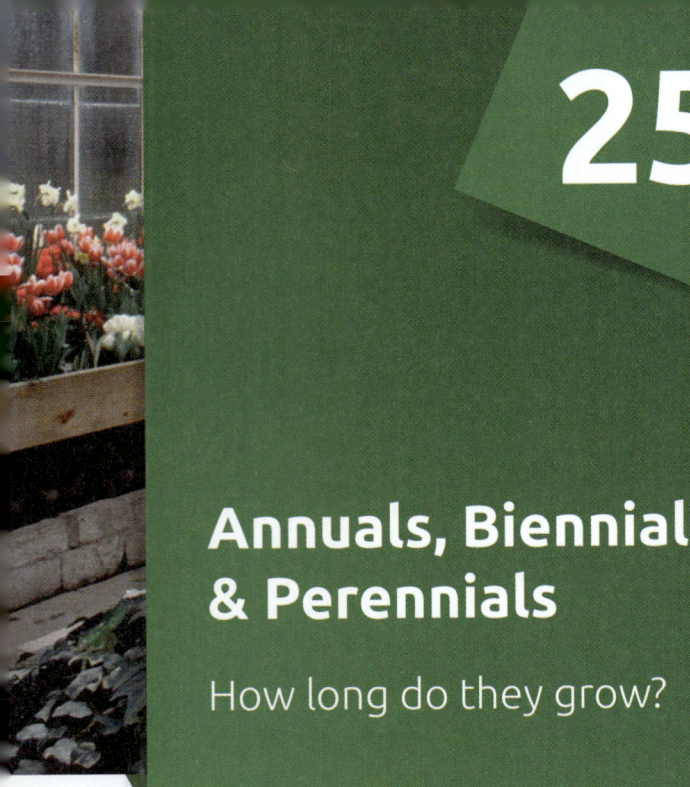

25

Annuals, Biennials, & Perennials

How long do they grow?

What is the life cycle of plants?

Words to know:

annual   perennial

biennial

Challenge words:

ephemeral

Every spring, plant nurseries, home improvement stores, and even supermarkets are filled with racks of flowering plants. And every spring, homeowners buy these plants to take home and put in their gardens and flowerpots. Why do we go through this yearly ritual? Why do we have to buy new plants each year? We do this because different plants have different lengths of life cycles.

Annuals are plants that live for only one growing season. These are mostly what you see for sale each spring. Annuals grow from seed, to mature plant, to flowers with ripe seeds in only a few months. At the end of the summer or fall, the plants produce seeds, wither, and die. These plants do not grow again. Therefore, to have the same beautiful flowers next year, many people buy new plants in the spring. Some popular annuals include petunias, marigolds, and zinnias.

In addition to many decorative flowers, most crops are annuals as well. Peas, beans, and grains complete their life cycles in one growing season. Most food crops are planted as seeds in the spring and harvested in the fall. These plants were designed by God to provide food for people living in climates that are not suitable for plant growth year round.

Annual

Flowers & Fruits

Biennial

Perennial

Some plants, however, do not complete their life cycles in only one season. Some plants require two growing seasons to produce seeds. These plants are called **biennials**. During the first season, biennials grow relatively small plants and store most of the food that is produced in its roots, stems, or leaves. The next year, the plant uses the stored food to help produce flowers and eventually seeds. Some common biennials include carrots, beets, and cabbages. We usually harvest these biennials after the first season so we can eat the plants and benefit from the stored food. Therefore, we often do not see the flowers of these plants. However, if we allow the plants to grow a second year we will see the flowers and seeds that are necessary for reproduction.

Finally, some plants continue to grow year after year. These plants are called **perennials**. Perennials grow and produce flowers and seeds each year. During the winter, many of these plants either rest or appear to die, but new growth occurs in the spring from the roots and stems of the plant. Trees and shrubs are the most common perennials. Other perennials include most wildflowers, peonies, and asparagus.

What did we learn?

- What is an annual plant?
- What is a biennial plant?
- What is a perennial plant?

Taking it further

- Why don't we often see the flowers of biennial plants?
- Why don't people grow new plants from the seeds produced by the annuals each year?

Plant word search

Complete the "Plant Word Search."

Flowers & Fruits

🏅 Ephemerals

Some plants have a very short life cycle. They may complete their full life cycles in as little as six weeks. These plants are called ephemerals, which means transitory or quickly fading. Ephemerals grow very quickly, produce flowers and seeds, and then die all within just a few short weeks. Why do you suppose God created some plants with the ability to go through their life cycles so quickly?

Many ephemerals are found in the desert where growing conditions are very harsh. These plants remain in seed dormancy for very long periods of time. However, when rain comes, these seeds suddenly spring to life and the plants grow very quickly. The water will not last long so plants cannot survive if they require months to mature.

Another place where a short growing season is required is on the woodland floor. During the summer, the leaves of the trees prevent most of the sunlight from reaching the forest floor, so most plants cannot grow there during the summer. But in the spring, before the trees leaf out, there is abundant sunshine on the forest floor. This is when many ephemeral plants grow. They only have a few weeks of sunshine, and God has designed them to complete their life cycle very quickly.

Some plants have a short life cycle and can complete several life cycles in one growing season. Most of these plants are considered weeds and can be very annoying, especially to farmers. The Bible says that weeds are a result of the curse placed on the earth at the Fall of man (see Genesis 3:17–19). So you see there are several reasons why some plants have very short life cycles.

These trilliums are spring ephemerals.

UNIT 6

Unusual Plants

◊ **Describe** the unique features of carnivorous plants.

◊ **Explain** the different tropisms and how they benefit plants.

◊ **Describe** how various plants are adapted to harsh environments.

◊ **Describe** how plants reproduce without seeds.

◊ **Explain** why algae and fungi are not plants.

26

Meat-eating Plants

Will it eat me?

How do plants eat insects?

Words to know:

carnivorous

Have you ever seen a Venus flytrap? This is a plant that traps an insect between special leaves and slowly digests it. But the Venus flytrap is not the only **carnivorous**, or meat-eating, plant. There are several types of plants that trap and digest small animals, usually insects.

Meat-eating plants are green plants that have chlorophyll and perform photosynthesis. So why do they also eat insects? Most meat-eating plants live in wet boggy soil that does not have enough nutrients. They trap insects to supplement their diet. This is a little bit like taking a vitamin pill.

Carnivorous plants have various ways to trap their meals. The sundew has leaves that are covered with short sticky hairs. When an insect lands on the leaf, it becomes stuck and the leaf slowly curls around it. Pitcher plants have long tube-shaped leaves, similar in shape to a trumpet. The rim of the pitcher produces nectar to attract insects. When the insect stops to sample the nectar it slips inside the pitcher and is then trapped by slippery walls and downward pointing hairs at the bottom.

The Venus flytrap (above) is designed with special leaves that work a little like a mousetrap. When

A sundew curling around an insect

Fun Fact

There are five carnivorous plants that are native to the United States: pitcher plant, bladderwort, butterwort, sundew, and Venus flytrap.

Unusual Plants

A pitcher plant with trapped bees

an insect lands on the special leaf, it moves the trigger bristles, which signal the leaf to begin closing. The leaves are edged with teeth-like spikes that quickly close around the insect preventing it from escaping.

Once the insect is trapped in one of these plants, the plant secretes an acid that begins to digest the insect's body. It may take several days to digest the insect. The plant cannot digest the exoskeleton—the hard outer shell of the insect. When it is done digesting the rest of the insect, it may open its leaves to let the wind blow the exoskeleton away. Most of the time, however, the exoskeleton remains in the trap and attracts unwary spiders. (You can learn more about carniverous plants by visiting the God's Design for Science Online Resource Page at answers-ingenesis.org/go/godsdesignlinks.)

🧠 What did we learn?

- What is a carnivorous plant?
- Why do some plants need to be carnivorous?
- How does a carnivorous plant eat an insect?

🚀 Taking it further

- Where are you likely to find carnivorous plants?
- How might a Venus flytrap tell the difference between an insect on its leaf and a raindrop?

Fun Fact

The largest carnivorous plants are in the genus *Nepenthes*. These large vines can grow over 30 feet (9 m) long. These tropical pitcher plants have traps designed to capture some of the largest prey, including creatures as large as frogs. Very rarely, captures of birds or rodents have been reported.

⚗️ Making a trap

In this activity, you will design a trap. The simplest trap is one where one end of a box is propped up by a stick. The prey knocks over the stick and is trapped in the box. You can make a simple trap like this or may design a more elaborate trap. You can use a small toy as the insect and pretend to catch the insect inside your trap.

Discuss how the trap works and how it is similar and different from the plant traps described in the lesson.

Unusual Plants

Cobra lily

One of the most interesting looking carnivorous plants is the cobra lily. The cobra lily is not a true lily but a pitcher plant. Special leaves grow up and bend over to form a pitcher that resembles the head of a cobra. It even grows leaves that resemble a tongue.

When an insect lands on the "tongue" it is attracted by the scent of nectar and crawls up the tongue inside the pitcher. The top of the pitcher has several windows that allow light to pass through. When the insect is ready to leave it usually flies toward the light thinking it is an exit, but instead of escaping, it hits the top of the pitcher. This knocks the insect into the neck of the pitcher, which is lined with downward

Cobra lily

facing hairs and a slippery fluid. It quickly becomes trapped and is digested by the plant.

Most carnivorous plants produce enzymes that digest the bodies of the insects that become trapped. But the cobra lily does not produce these enzymes. Instead, it relies on bacteria to break down the bodies of its prey and then absorbs the nutrients.

Cobra lilies grow in swampy mountain bogs in southwestern Oregon and northern California. If you were to design a carnivorous plant what would it look like? How would it trap insects or other animals? Use your imagination and draw a picture of your meat-eating plant. Be sure to give it a name.

Parasites & Passengers

Living off of each other

How do parasitic plants survive?

Words to know:

parasite	passenger plant
host	vine

Although most plants around us live and grow the way we have discussed in the previous lessons, a few do not. Some plants are **parasites**. This means that they obtain the water, minerals, and food they need by stealing them from other plants. Parasitic plants often have roots when they are young, but once they tap into another plant those roots wither and the plant gets all of its nourishment from the **host** plant.

Parasites attach themselves to the host using special organs called *haustoria*, which are suckers that penetrate into the stem or roots of the host so it can suck the liquids from the host plant. Some common parasitic plants include mistletoe, dodder, and eyebright.

Some plants live and grow on other plants without tapping into them or harming them in any way. These plants are called passengers. **Passenger plants** are found most commonly on trees. These plants usually grow on trees in order to have better access to sunlight. Many passenger plants grow in the trees of the rain forest.

One passenger plant is the moth orchid. These orchids are often found in the branches of trees in the

Spanish moss is a passenger plant.

Unusual Plants

Moth orchid on a tree

rain forests. They have three kinds of roots. One kind of root anchors the plant to the host. The second kind of root is an aerial root that absorbs water directly from the air. And the third kind of root absorbs minerals from its surroundings. These orchids produce flowers that produce seeds. The seeds are scattered by the wind and blown into the bark of other trees where they germinate and grow new plants.

Unlike the moth orchid, which is fairly large, most passenger plants are small. The most common passenger plants in North America are mosses and lichens.

Similarly, **vines** are plants that use other plants for support, but they have their own root systems. One common vine is the wild grape. As birds eat the fruit, they deposit the seeds near trees as they rest in the branches. The seed sprouts and the vine begins to grow up the side of a tree, spreading its leaves out as it grows. Vines can also grow up the sides of buildings or cliffs or on trellises in gardens. Poison ivy vines also have small aerial roots that make them look fuzzy. Other vines include true ivy vines, honeysuckle, pole beans, and Virginia creeper.

Parasite model

Purpose: To demonstrate how a parasite steals nutrients from a host

Materials: soda straw, knife, coffee stirrer or small straw

Procedure:

1. Cut a small hole in the side near the center of a soda straw. The hole should be the same size as a coffee stirrer or smaller straw.

2. Insert a coffee stirrer into the hole so that the edge is in the center of the straw. Angle the coffee stirrer so that it is pointing slightly down—not straight out to the side. This stirrer represents the haustoria, or suckers, that the parasitic plant sends into the host plant.

3. Place the straw under running water in a sink.

Conclusion: Observe how most of the water flows out of the bottom of the straw but some of the water flows out of the coffee stirrer. This smaller amount of water represents the nutrients that would flow into the parasitic plant.

Search for parasites & passengers

If possible, go outside and search for parasitic plants and passenger plants. Large trees are the most likely place to locate these types of plants. Look for mistletoe, lichen, and moss. Mistletoe is a common parasite. Lichen and moss are passengers. Poison ivy, honeysuckle, and Virginia creeper are vines. If you find something growing on a tree, closely observe how it is growing. Is it attached to the outside only, or does part of the plant penetrate into the stem?

A field guide is useful in helping you identify the plants you find. *Reader's Digest North American Wildlife* is a good resource to have available anytime you explore nature. Many other field guides are available at your library as well.

Unusual Plants

Fun Fact

Mistletoe, considered sacred by the British Druids, was believed to have many miraculous powers. Among the Romans, it was a symbol of peace, and it was said that when enemies met under it, they discarded their arms and declared a truce. From this comes our Christmas custom of kissing under the mistletoe. England was the first country to use it during the Christmas season.

What did we learn?

- What is a parasitic plant?
- What is a passenger plant?
- How do passenger plants obtain water and minerals?

Taking it further

- Where is the most likely place to find passenger plants?
- Do passenger plants perform photosynthesis?
- Do parasitic plants perform photosynthesis?

Plant research

There are many interesting parasitic and passenger plants. Choose one of the plants from the following lists, or another parasitic or passenger that you are interested in, and find out all you can. You may want to search the Internet for epiphytic plants, which is the scientific name for passenger plants.

Draw a picture of your plant and its host or find photos of the actual plant. Make a presentation to your class or family, telling them what you learned.

Parasites
- Mistletoe
- Rafflesia
- Dodder
- Love Vine

Passengers
- Moth orchid
- Spanish moss
- Lichen
- Old man's beard

Unusual Plants

Tropisms

How plants respond

How does a plant know which way to grow?

Words to know:

tropism	hydrotropism
geotropism	heliotropism/ phototropism

Challenge words:

positive tropism	thermotropism
negative tropism	thigmotropism
chemotropism	

Do seeds grow if they are planted upside down? Will a plant grow if it is far from the river or other water source? How can a plant survive if something blocks the light? God has designed plants so they know how to grow. The earth gives clues to the plants to help them survive. These "survival techniques" are called tropisms (from a Greek word meaning "turning"). A **tropism** is a response by the plant to a certain stimulus or condition. Plants experience several tropisms.

Geotropism—Roots always grow down and out and stems always grow up from a seed regardless of which direction it is planted in the ground. The plant knows how to do this because it responds to the pull of gravity. If a plant in a pot gets knocked

These trees were knocked over when young and then began to grow straight up again. This is an example of geotropism.

Plants turn toward light sources to maximize photosynthesis.

leaf, some cells contract and others expand to turn the leaf toward the sun. As the sun moves through the sky, the leaves follow it. If something blocks the sun, the plant will grow toward any available light, allowing it to bypass whatever may be in its way. These are responses to light.

God designed plants with these abilities to increase their chances of survival. Tropisms demonstrate God's brilliant design.

over so that the roots and stem are now sideways, after a few days the roots will begin growing downward and the stem will begin growing upward again in response to gravity.

Hydrotropism—Roots can sense water and will grow towards it. Some plants, willows for example, can send roots more than 30 feet (9 m) sideways to reach a source of water. Dicots with taproots often go down 20–30 feet (6–9 m) to find water.

Heliotropism (also called **phototropism**)— Leaves turn to face the sun to obtain the maximum energy for photosynthesis. As the sun hits a

What did we learn?

- What is geotropism?
- What is hydrotropism?
- What is phototropism or heliotropism?

🚀 Taking it further

- Why are tropisms sometimes called "survival techniques"?
- Will a seed germinate if it is planted 5 feet (1.5 m) from the water?
- Where are some places you would not want to plant water-seeking plants such as willows?

🧪 Observing heliotropism

Purpose: To observe phototropism/heliotropism

Materials: house plant

Procedure:

1. Place a houseplant near a window. Observe which direction the leaves are facing.

2. After a day or two, observe the plant again. You should be able to see that the leaves are all facing toward the window.

3. Turn the plant 180 degrees and leave it for another two days.

4. Observe the leaves again. They will have turned around to face the window again.

Unusual Plants

ⓜ More tropisms

Tropism is the response of a plant to a certain stimulus. **Positive tropism** means that the plant moves toward the stimulus; **negative tropism** means the plant moves away from the stimulus. Hydrotropism is a positive tropism because the roots of the plant move toward the water. Phototropism or heliotropism is also a positive tropism because leaves move toward the light and stems grow toward the light. Geotropism is positive for the roots and negative for the stems because the roots move toward the pull of gravity and the stems move away from the pull of gravity.

In addition to these responses, other tropisms have been observed in certain plants. **Chemotropism** is a response to chemicals. In many flowering plants, the pollination process is a positive chemotropism. The ovary releases a chemical. This causes the pollen tube to move toward it. This completes the pollination process.

Thermotropism is a response to heat or cold. Some leaves will curl up when the air around them becomes cold. This is a negative tropism. Some plants have roots that respond to heat. When the soil above the plant becomes warm the roots move toward the heat, but when it becomes too hot, the roots move away from the heat.

Some plants also experience **thigmotropism**, which is a response to touch. Can you think of any plants that we have studied that respond to touch? Tendrils have a positive response to touch. They curl around solid objects that they come in contact with. Plant roots on the other hand have negative thigmotropism. As roots grow they move away from something solid. This allows the roots to find spaces between the bits of dirt and more easily penetrate the soil.

Complete the "Tropisms" worksheet by drawing a picture demonstrating each tropism listed.

Grape vine tendrils coil and latch on for support. This is an example of thigmotropism.

29

Survival Techniques

Surviving in harsh climates

How can plants survive in harsh conditions?

Words to know:

succulent

Plants can be found growing in nearly every part of the world. But all climates are not necessarily conducive to plant growth. Some climates have too much or too little water. Some climates are very hot or very cold. But God designed plants that can grow in even these very harsh climates. In addition to tropisms, God has given these plants special survival techniques to help them deal with the harsh conditions.

We have learned how some plants that grow where there are few nitrates due to too much water can supplement their "diet" by digesting insects. Conversely, plants that live where there is very little water have been designed to make the most of what water is available. These plants are called **succulents** and can often go for weeks or even months without water. When water is available, the cactus and other succulents absorb as much water as they can, storing it in their fleshy stems. They are designed with ridges in their stems that can expand to hold more water when it is available.

Also, to keep the water from evaporating, cacti have needle-like leaves with very little surface area so water does not evaporate quickly. The cactus's needles also help keep animals from eating its stem and taking its water.

Other plants have been designed to survive in alpine areas where there is often high wind, cold temperatures, and little available water. These alpine plants are small and grow low to the ground to survive the wind. They often grow in dense groups to provide protection and insulation to the whole group of plants. When summer comes to the high mountain areas, these plants

Alpine plants are small and grow low to the ground.

Unusual Plants

Fun Fact

The cardón cactus is the world's largest cactus. It is found in the American southwest, mostly in Baja California. Some of the largest cardónes have been measured at nearly 70 feet (21 m) high and weigh up to 25 tons.

bloom and reproduce very quickly to take advantage of the short growing season. Also, many alpine plants have tiny hairs on their leaves to protect them from the intense sun at high altitudes. These hairs can also act as insulation to protect the leaves from extreme cold.

Each of these plants shows the wonder of God's design and His provision for all parts of His creation.

 What did we learn?

- How do some plants survive in hot dry climates?
- How do some plants survive in cold windy climates?

Taking it further

- Why do alpine plants need protection from the sun?

Examining a cactus

Carefully examine a small cactus. Using a magnifying glass, examine the needles and the fleshy stem. Look for folds in the stem that might expand to hold more water or shrink when water is not available. Discuss how this plant was designed to survive in the harsh climate of a desert.

Designed for survival

In order to survive, plants require many different things. You will appreciate all of the ways God has designed plants for survival when you complete the "Designed for Survival" worksheet.

We have talked about many different ways that plants have been designed to survive in various conditions. Review the lessons in this book for ideas to put on the worksheet. You can start with the designs listed in this lesson, but there are many more listed throughout the previous lessons.

Unusual Plants

Reproduction without Seeds

There are other ways.

How can a plant reproduce without seeds?

Words to know:

vegetative reproduction   rhizome

vegetative propagation

Challenge words:

cloning   cutting

grafting   genetic modification

rootstock   GMO

scion

Some plants that reproduce by producing seeds can also reproduce in other ways as well. A small piece of the plant can be used to start a new plant. This is called **vegetative reproduction** or **vegetative propagation**. There are several ways that vegetative reproduction can take place. One way is when a plant sends out special creeping stems called stolons. This is the main way that gardeners get new strawberry plants. After the plant is done producing fruit, it sends out runners, or stolons, that grow new plants at the end of the runners.

Many plants that bloom in the early spring, such as tulips or crocuses, grow from bulbs. Bulbs often produce new bulbs underground that can be used to grow new plants. Some plants, such as the iris, grow **rhizomes**, special stems that grow

Fun Fact

The creosote plant that grows in the American southwest reproduces vegetatively. It is believed that some of the creosote plants growing today have the exact same genetic make-up as plants that were growing thousands of years ago.

Some plants reproduce by sending out creeping stems called stolons.

Unusual Plants

Unearthed bamboo rhizomes

can be placed in soil. Although seeds are the primary way to get new plants, vegetative reproduction is often used because it can have faster results. 🌱

underground, and produce new plants. Other special underground stems are tubers. Potatoes are tubers and new potato plants can be started from a small part of a potato.

Finally, some plants reproduce by growing new roots from a cut stem or leaf. Ivy and many other houseplants can be cut and placed in water to encourage new roots to grow. Then the new plant

What did we learn?

- What are some ways that plants can reproduce without growing from seeds?

Taking it further

- Why can a potato grow from a piece of potato instead of from a seed?

- Will the new plant be just like the original plant?

Growing a new potato plant

Purpose: To grow a new potato plant without using seeds

Materials: a potato with "eyes"—small white growths on the side of the potato, jar, potting soil

Procedure:

1. Cut out a square of the potato around the eye.

2. Plant this part of the potato in a jar filled with potting soil. It should be planted about two inches below the surface.

3. Keep the soil moist but not too wet.

4. In 10 to 14 days, you will see a potato plant begin to grow from the piece of the original potato.

Unusual Plants

Cloning plants

Most plants reproduce sexually by the uniting of pollen and ovule to produce a seed. When this happens, DNA from the plant producing the pollen unites with DNA from the plant producing the ovule and the resulting seed has unique DNA that is a combination of the parent plants' DNA. God designed plants to reproduce this way so that problems that occur in the DNA are not as likely to be passed on to the next generation.

When plants experience vegetative reproduction, the new plant has the exact DNA as the plant that it came from. When a strawberry plant sends out runners, the new plants will have the same DNA as the parent plants. When the potato eye that you planted grows a new potato plant it will have the same DNA as the potato plant that the potato came from. This is a form of cloning. Cloning is producing offspring with identical DNA to the parent. This form of reproduction occurs naturally in some plants. Cloning is also used in many areas of agriculture.

One of the most widespread uses of vegetative reproduction in agriculture is in fruit tree reproduction. Although sexual reproduction keeps plants healthy, the fruit is different from one plant to the next. This is okay in the wild, but people expect a golden delicious apple to taste like a golden delicious apple. They do not want it to taste like a Granny Smith apple or a sour wild apple. Growing fruit trees from seed can have unexpected results. Therefore, commercial tree growers use vegetative reproduction to produce clone trees that produce fruit with the desired qualities.

The most common form of vegetative reproduction used to grow new fruit trees is grafting. The first part of grafting is growing the rootstock. Usually, roots and a stem are taken from an existing root structure to form a new rootstock. Sometimes trees are grown from seeds to produce new rootstock. The rootstock is chosen for its hardiness and ability to support the tree that will be grafted to it, not for its fruit.

Once the rootstock is ready, a stem or a bud, referred as a scion (SI-un), is cut from the desired tree and a cut is made in the rootstock. The cut side of the bud is placed next to the cut in the rootstock and the two pieces are taped together and the cut is sealed with grafting wax. With the cambium cells of both plants next to each other, the two plants begin to grow together. This completes the grafting process. What results is a tree that produces fruit that is identical to the tree that the bud came from.

Other plants are propagated by a process called cutting. This is a very simple process. A stem or branch from one plant is cut off and placed in soil. The cutting grows roots and becomes a new plant genetically identical to the original. Forsythia bushes are often propagated in this way.

Cloning ensures that each new plant is genetically identical to its parent; however, sometimes it is desirable to make a plant that is very different from its parent plant. Scientists have developed ways to modify the genes in the DNA in particular plants to obtain new plants with different characteristics. This practice is called genetic modification. Although people have been breeding plants to get desired results for centuries, the idea of actually modifying the DNA is a relatively new one. Plants that have been developed by genetic modification are called genetically modified organisms or GMOs.

Do some research to find out how genetic modification works, how it is being used, what foods you might be eating that are GMOs, and what controversies surround this interesting field of science. Be sure to share what you learn with someone else.

The grafts can be clearly seen on these almond trees.

Ferns

Seedless plants

How do ferns reproduce?

Words to know:

frond

spore

Challenge words:

fiddlehead

Not all plants have flowers and produce seeds. Plants without seeds include ferns and mosses. Ferns are similar to other plants because they have roots, stems, vascular tissue, and leaves with chlorophyll. These leaves are called **fronds**. But ferns do not have flowers or seeds.

So how do ferns reproduce? Ferns produce microscopic **spores** on the backs of their leaves. These spores do not contain a baby plant like a seed does. They contain just enough information to grow a tiny leaf-like structure, which then produces

Fun Fact

A typical fern plant may produce up to one billion spores per year.

an egg and sperm which, when united, form the beginnings of a new fern plant. This method of reproduction is very different from the way most plants reproduce; therefore, ferns are classified separately from most other plants.

Young ferns

Fun Fact

One of the first plants to begin growing after a volcanic eruption is the fern. The big island of Hawaii has many beautiful fern forests growing where lava once covered the ground.

Unusual Plants

Ferns generally need a lot of water so they usually grow in areas with lots of rain. Ferns are generally small plants but a few grow up to 60 feet (18 m) tall in the rain forests.

What did we learn?

- How are ferns like other plants?
- What are fern leaves called?
- How are ferns different from other plants?
- How do they reproduce?

Taking it further

- Why can't ferns reproduce with seeds?

🧪 Fern fronds

Closely examine this picture, showing fern fronds with spores on the back. Then paint a picture of a fern frond. After the paint is dry, glue small amounts of corn meal or sand on the frond to represent the spores.

If you have a fern plant available, place a frond on the table, cover it with a piece of paper, and color back and forth over it with a crayon to make a tracing, or rubbing, of the leaf. Then glue the corn meal onto your rubbing to show the spores.

🏅 Fern structure

Although ferns have many of the same structures that are found in other plants, they do not grow the way that most plants grow. Instead of having a vertical stem, most ferns have a horizontal stem called a rhizome. The rhizomes grow just below the surface. As in most plants, the roots grow down from the stems.

Since the stems of the fern plant are underground, the fronds, or leaves, grow up from the ground. They start out as a small rolled up structure called a **fiddlehead**, which is actually the developing petiole of the frond. As it grows, the fiddlehead unrolls and develops into a frond.

Ferns are abundant in the fossil record showing that in the past ferns covered much of the earth. Fern fossils are often found in coal beds. These fossils are nearly identical to ferns found today, showing that ferns have not changed or evolved. Also, many of

Mature fern

Rhizome

Unusual Plants

Fossil ferns are identical to modern ferns.

A fiddlehead

the fossilized ferns clearly show the beautiful lacy texture of a living frond, indicating that the leaves were covered quickly while the plant was still alive, not slowly as evolutionary theories indicate. This is consistent with the idea of plants becoming buried quickly during the worldwide Flood in Genesis.

Add ground, rhizomes, and roots to your painting to show the whole structure of a fern plant.

32

Mosses

Do you really find moss on the north side of trees?

How do mosses grow and reproduce?

Challenge words:

peat

Another group of non seed-bearing plants

is mosses. These are tiny plants with thin, green leaves, stems, and root-like structures. Most mosses absorb more water through their leaves than through their roots. Mosses do not have flowers or seeds. They reproduce with spores in a similar way to that of ferns.

Fun Fact

Most animals don't eat lichens—they are hard to digest and have little nutritional value. But reindeer eat lots of them. Why? A certain lichen, called *reindeer moss*, contains a chemical that helps a reindeer's cells keep working at low temperatures. When the reindeer make their yearly journey across the icy Arctic region, this chemical keeps them from freezing, just like antifreeze keeps a car from freezing up in the cold winter.

Mosses have two stages in their life cycles. One stage is the green moss plant stage with which you are probably familiar. The second stage is the capsule and stalk stage. In this stage, the plant produces a stalk like a thin stem with a capsule on the end. This capsule produces the spores that later produce new moss plants.

Most mosses are very small, but they can grow in large clumps or groups. Mosses are found wherever there is a consistently wet environment. The

Unusual Plants

idea that moss always grows on the north side of a tree comes from the fact that in winter sun shines on the south side, making it warmer and dryer and therefore less likely to grow moss. But the truth is that moss will grow anywhere that is wet enough. Mosses love bogs and swamps, but will also grow in forests and even in the tundra.

What did we learn?

- How do mosses differ from seed-bearing plants?
- How do mosses differ from ferns?
- How do mosses produce food?

Taking it further

- Are you likely to find moss in a desert? Why/why not?

Find the moss

Using art supplies, draw pictures of a forest or swamp. Then glue dried moss in the places you are most likely to find it. Be sure to include the bases of trees, under rocks, or on fallen logs.

After making the pictures, go out in your yard and search for moss. Look under rocks, on old logs, or in damp shady areas. Use a magnifying glass to observe the small leaves.

Peat moss

One of the most important mosses is called sphagnum moss. Sphagnum moss, also called peat moss, has leaf-like structures that can absorb and hold water. This gives peat moss a spongy texture. This is important for many reasons. First, this moss helps prevent soil erosion by quickly absorbing rain water that would otherwise wash away soil. When peat moss dies, it is used as a soil additive to increase the ability of the soil to hold water. Many people add peat moss to the soil when planting trees and other plants to help keep moisture near the roots of the new plants.

Peat moss grows primarily in swampy bogs. As it begins to decay it becomes compressed by the weight of the water and other plants. These layers are called **peat**. The acid in the moss prevents it from completely decaying, so in certain bogs the peat is several feet thick. In Ireland and other areas, people cut squares of peat from the bogs, dry them and use them as fuel.

Peat moss and many other mosses are also important in the formation of soil. The plants secrete an acid that helps to break down the minerals in rocks. This helps create new soil and to add minerals to the soil. This is just one way that God designed the world to be able to sustain life.

Blocks of peat drying in Scotland

Purpose: To demonstrate the water absorbing qualities of peat moss

Materials: peat moss, three paper cups, dirt, water

Procedure:

1. Place ½ cup of peat moss in a paper cup.

2. Place a ½ cup of dirt from your yard in a second cup.

3. Place ¼ cup of peat moss and ¼ cup of dirt together in a third cup and stir the dirt and peat moss together.

4. Pour ¼ cup of water into each sample.

5. Let the water sink in then feel the texture/moisture of each sample.

6. Wait 1 hour then feel the texture and moisture of each sample again. Which samples are still moist?

7. Test the samples again after 1 more hour. Which samples are moist now?

8. See if any of the samples are still moist after 24 hours.

Conclusion: What difference did adding peat moss make to the ability of the soil to hold water? You should find that the peat moss and the soil with the peat moss mixed in both held the moisture longer than the dirt by itself. This is why many people add peat moss to their soil.

Unusual Plants

33

Algae

Are all green things plants?

Why are algae important organisms?

Words to know:

algae

primary consumer

secondary consumer

diatom

Challenge words:

filament

carrageenin

algin

Have you ever walked along a lake or pond and noticed green scum on the top of the water? Or maybe you have seen an area in the ocean that is a different color from the rest of the water. Have you ever pulled long, green, stringy material from a pond or stream or seaweed from the ocean? If so, then you have seen algae.

Algae are plantlike organisms that generally live in the water. They do not have roots, leaves, stems, flowers, or seeds so they are not truly plants. They contain chlorophyll and produce their own food, like plants, but are classified in the kingdom Protista.

Algae are very important organisms. They provide food for many fish and other sea creatures.

They are the beginning of most aquatic food chains. Nearly everything in the ocean eats algae or eats something that has eaten algae. Animals that eat algae or plants are called **primary consumers**. Animals that eat other animals that have eaten algae or plants are called **secondary consumers**.

In addition to food, algae are used in a variety of manufactured products. **Diatoms** are yellow algae that have silica in their cell walls. Large deposits of dead diatoms have been found and are used in toothpastes, scouring powders, tiles, and bricks. Diatom deposits are also used in explosives to help

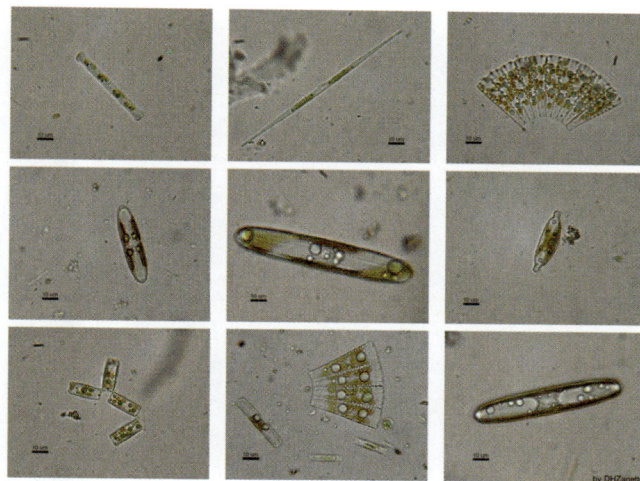

Microscopic images of common freshwater diatoms

Algae are used as wrappers for sushi.

stabilize the explosive material. Algae are used in many food products including wrappers for sushi and other oriental foods and as thickeners in ice cream, pudding, and salad dressings.

Most important of all, algae produce more than half of the oxygen in the world. Algae are the most abundant life form on Earth, with the exception of bacteria, thriving in the surface layer of the oceans. Scientists believe they perform as much as 70% of all photosynthesis in the world. This makes algae one of the most beneficial organisms on Earth.

What did we learn?

- Why are algae such important organisms?
- What gives algae its green color?

Taking it further

- Why are some algae yellow, brown, blue, or red?

 Food chain picture

Scientists often talk about food chains. There were not any food chains in God's original creation since all animals (and man) ate only plants (Genesis 1:29–30). However, after the Fall of man, animals began to eat each other. Today, food chains begin with plants or algae. Animals eat the plants. Then other animals eat those animals and so on. Most aquatic food chains begin with algae. In one food chain, algae are eaten by microscopic animals such as rotifers. The rotifers are eaten by tiny fish such as minnows. The minnows are eaten by perch, and the perch are eaten by birds.

Purpose: To illustrate a food chain

Materials: colored pencils, construction paper, scissors

Procedure:

1. Draw a picture of a lake using colored pencils.

2. Cut out different animals in the food chain from construction paper.

3. Glue the animals on the picture in the order that they occur in the food chain. Be sure to make an area of the lake greenish where the algae are and start your food chain in that location.

4. Identify the primary and secondary consumers of the algae.

Amazing algae

Algae are generally classified by their color. There are green, yellow, brown, and red algae. All algae contain chlorophyll, which is green. But many algae contain other pigments as well, giving them different colors. The green algae comprise the largest group of algae. Many green algae live as single cells, but others connect together. If several cells connect end to end they are called a **filament**. Other green algae survive in large groups called colonies. Spirogyra is one of the most common filament algae. These algae form long green threads. Inside each cell is a spiral shaped chloroplast which performs photosynthesis. Spirogyra can be found in nearly any pond.

You have already learned about yellow algae called diatoms which contain silica. Brown algae are often called seaweed. We generally think of algae as being very small, and most are microscopic; however, the brown algae are multi-cellular and can be up to 200 feet long. Kelp is the largest algae. The longest kelp ever recorded was 10.5 miles (17 km) long. Kelp is also one of the most useful brown algae. It contains a substance called algin which is used in making many products including chocolate milk, ice cream, mayonnaise, and lotions. **Algin** is a sticky substance in kelp that helps to keep these products smooth and creamy.

A few seaweeds are red algae. Red algae is also useful in manufacturing different products. **Carrageenin** is a gelatin-like substance found in many red algae that is used to thicken different foods including some ice cream. Red algae is also used to make agar, which is the medium that scientists use to

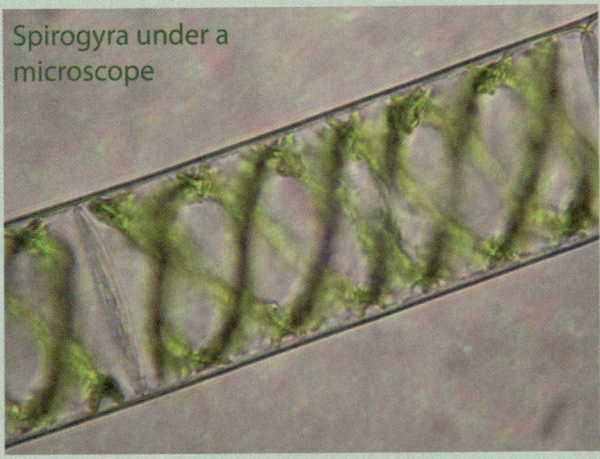

Spirogyra under a microscope

A kelp bed

grow bacteria in the laboratory.

As you can see, in addition to producing the majority of the oxygen in the world, algae are very useful in many commercial applications. You can view algae yourself if you have a microscope.

Purpose: To examine pond water for algae

Materials: pond water, microscope

Procedure:

1. Obtain a sample of pond water and examine it with a microscope. You will likely find several types of algae, but you are almost certain to see spirogyra, which are easily recognizable by their long green chains.

2. Draw pictures of any algae that you see and try to identify them.

Unusual Plants

34

Fungi

Are these really plants?

Are fungi plants?

Words to know:

fungi

What makes an organism a plant? The accepted definition of a plant is something that can create its own food through photosynthesis and has the tissues to make roots, stems, and leaves. By this definition, fungi are not plants. **Fungi** are classified in their own kingdom and include mushrooms, toadstools, molds, yeasts, and mildews.

Because fungi do not have chlorophyll, they must take nutrients from other plants or animals and convert them into food. Most fungi reproduce by spores or by budding.

Many fungi can be harmful. Many are poisonous. You must be especially careful when eating mushrooms. Never eat wild mushrooms or mushrooms that come from someplace other than a food store as they may cause serious illness or even death. Some fungi spoil our food. Have you ever grabbed a loaf of bread or a bag of bagels from your cupboard only to find that mold was growing on the food? Some fungi cause diseases such as athlete's foot. And others, such as corn smut, damage crops.

Unusual Plants

Fun Fact

The ancient Egyptians are believed to be the first civilization to use yeast to make their bread rise. Aren't you glad they did? Otherwise, we might not have all those great sandwiches and bread rolls.

As bad as some of these fungi are, there are many more fungi that are useful to people. Some mushrooms are good for food. Yeast is used to make our bread fluffy. Some molds are used to make medicine and save people's lives. Other molds are used to give cheeses their unique flavors. Finally, fungi aid in the decay of dead plants and animals. Without fungi and bacteria to aid in the decaying process, the world would soon be filled with dead plants and animals.

 # What did we learn?

- Why are fungi not considered plants and given their own kingdom?

- What are some good uses for fungi?

 # Taking it further

- What other conditions might affect mold growth other than those tested here?

- How can you keep your bread from becoming moldy?

Grow that mold

Purpose: To better understand the conditions that foster mold growth

Materials: six pieces of bread (homemade bread or bread without preservatives works best), three plastic sandwich bags, "Mold Data Sheet."

Procedure:

1. Place one slice of bread in each of the 3 sandwich bags and seal the bags.

2. Place one slice of bread without a bag and one slice in a bag in a warm dry area such as a cupboard in the kitchen.

3. Place one slice of bread without a bag and one slice in a bag in a cold area such as the refrigerator.

4. Place the remaining slices in a moist area such as a bathroom.

5. Now, make a hypothesis (an educated guess) about which slices you expect to see mold grow on. What are

the reasons for your hypothesis? Write your hypothesis at the top of the "Mold Data Sheet."

6. Observe each slice of bread once a day for several days until you see significant mold growth. Write your observations on the "Mold Data Sheet" each day.

7. After several days, review the hypothesis and see if you got the results you expected. Why was your hypothesis correct or incorrect?

🎖 Spore print

Mushrooms reproduce by spores. The spores are produced in the cap of the mushroom. You can view these spores if you make a spore print. It is fun and interesting to make spore prints.

Purpose: To observe the spores produced by a mushroom.

Materials: fresh mushroom, knife, index card, hair spray

Procedure:

1. Cut the stem of the mushroom off and place the cap on an index card in a location that it will not be disturbed.

2. Leave the mushroom on the card overnight.

3. The next day, carefully remove the cap from the card. You will see the pattern of the ribs inside the cap. This pattern is made by the spores from inside the mushroom cap.

4. Carefully spray a light coat of aerosol hair spray over the print to preserve it. After the hair spray dries, you can pick up the card and examine the print in more detail.

Unusual Plants

35

Conclusion

Appreciating the world of plants

Thank God for plants.

God has created a wonderful world of plants. We look around us, and everywhere we see flowers, trees, bushes, and grass. When we eat, we are aware of God's provision as we see all of the fruits, vegetables, and grains that are available to eat everyday. Plants provides food, shelter, and clothing for us. Plants clean the air by recycling our exhaled carbon dioxide, and through photosynthesis they make food and produce oxygen. Thank God today for the wonderful world of plants!

Write a poem to express your wonder at God's design for the world of plants.

🧪 Plant collage

Purpose: To make a plant collage

Materials: dried leaves, flowers, grass, twigs, seeds, seed pods, cones, bark, etc.

Procedure:

1. Glue the plant materials to a piece of tag board and make a beautiful picture to remind you of God's wonderful world of plants.

Glossary

Adventitious roots   Roots that grow in unexpected places or in unexpected ways

Aerial roots   Roots that take water from the air

Aggregate fruit   Formed from one flower with multiple pistils and ovaries

Algae   Plantlike organisms that often live in the water; Kingdom Protista

Alternate leaf arrangement   One leaf grows from each node on alternating sides of the stem

Anatomy   The study of the human body

Angiosperm   Plant that reproduces with flowers, fruit, and seeds

Annual   Plant that completes life cycle in one growing season

Anther   Part of the stamen that produces pollen

Axillary bud/Lateral bud   Bud growing from side of stem

Bark   Dead, hardened epidermis cells in woody stems

Biennial   Plant that completes life cycle in two growing seasons

Binomial classification   Two-name system of classification developed by Carl Linnaeus

Botany   The study of plants

Cambium cells   Cells that divide to produce more xylem and phloem

Carnivorous   Meat eating

Catalyst   Substance that speeds up a chemical reaction

Cell   Smallest unit of an organism that can survive on its own

Cell membrane   Outer coating or "skin" of a cell

Cell wall   Rigid outermost layer of a plant cell

Cereal grass   Grains such as wheat and oats

Chlorophyll   Green substance in chloroplasts that makes photosynthesis possible

Chloroplast   Part of a cell that transforms sunlight into food (glucose)

Conifer   Plant that reproduces with seeds in cones

Cotyledon   Food stored in seed to supply nourishment to new plant

Cross-pollination   Flower is pollinated with pollen from another plant

Cuticle   Top layer of epidermis

Cytoplasm   Liquid that fills a cell

Deciduous   Trees that lose their leaves in the winter

Diatoms   Yellow algae with silica in their cell walls

Dicot   Seed with two cotyledons

Disperse/Dispersal   Movement of seed away from parent plant

Dormant   A condition in which the seed in inactive or "asleep"

Embryo   "Baby" plant inside a seed

Endosperm   Additional nutrients absorbed by cotyledon during germination of monocots

Epidermis   Outer layer of cells in a young stem

Evergreen   Trees that do not lose their leaves in the winter

Fibrous roots   Roots spread out in many directions

Filament   Stalk of the stamen that supports the anther

Flowers   Organs that produce fruits and seeds for reproduction

Forage grass   Taller grass eaten by grazing animals

Fronds   "Leaves" of a fern

Fruit   Ripened ovary

Fungi   Organisms that cannot make their own food including mushrooms and yeast; Kingdom Fungi

Geotropism   The ability to sense up and down, response to gravity

Germinate   When seeds begin to grow

Guard cells   Cells which open and close the stomata

Gymnosperm   Plant that reproduces with cones and seeds

Haustoria   Shoots sent from parasitic roots to tap into another plant's roots

Heartwood   Dead xylem cells in center of tree that no longer transport materials

Heliotropism/Phototropism   The ability to sense light; response to light

Herbaceous plants   Plants with bendable stems

Hilum   Location on seed where it was attached to the ovary of the plant

Host   Plant from which a parasite takes nutrients

Hydrotropism   The ability to sense water, response to water

Internode   Stem between two nodes

Kingdom   Group of living things that have broad common characteristics

Leaves   Organs that manufacture food for the plant

Mitochondria   Part of a cell that breaks down food into energy

Monocot   Seed with one cotyledon

Multiple fruit   Formed when several flowers form fruit that fuse together

Nectar   Sweet liquid that attracts pollinators

Node   Point where leaf attaches to stem

Nucleus   Control center or "brain" of a cell

Opposite leaf arrangement   Two leaves grow on opposite sides of the stem from one node

Organ   A group of tissues working together to perform a function

Ornamental grass   Very tall grass used for landscaping

Ovary   Part of the pistil that produces the ovules

Ovule   Unfertilized seed, egg

Palmate   Palm-like venation

Parasite   Plant that gains nutrients by tapping into and taking them from other plants

Parasitic roots   Roots that tap into another plant's roots to steal nutrients and water

Passenger plant   Attached to other plants but does not harm them

Perennial   Plant that grows year after year

Petal   Part of the flower that attracts pollinators—often brightly colored and scented

Petiole   The part of the leaf that attaches to the stem

Phloem   Tubes that transport food from leaves back down to the roots

Photosynthesis   Process that changes light, water, and carbon dioxide into sugar and oxygen

Phylum, class, order, family, genus, species   Different levels of how living things in a kingdom are divided into groups by common characteristics

Pinnate   Feather-like venation

Pistil   Female part of the flower—contains ovules

Pistillate   Flower that produces only pistils

Plumule   Part of embryo which develops into the stem and leaves

Pneumatophore   Roots that grow above ground to absorb oxygen from the air

Pollen   Fine powder needed for reproduction

Pollination   Uniting of pollen with an ovule

Pollinator   Animal that distributes pollen

Primary consumers   Animals that eat plants

Prop roots   Roots growing out from the side of a stem then into the ground to provide stability

Radicle   Part of the embryo which develops into the roots

Respiration   Exchange of oxygen and carbon dioxide in living cells

Rhizomes   Special underground stems that grow horizontally

Root cap   Covering that protects tip of root

Roots   Organs that anchor plants and absorb water and nutrients

Rosette leaf arrangement   Leaves grow from the bottom of the stem

Sapwood   Area of stem with active xylem and phloem cells

Secondary consumers   Animals that eat the primary consumers

Seed coat   Protective covering on outside of seed

Self-pollination   Flower is pollinated with pollen from the same plant

Sepal   Part of the flower that protects the developing flower

Shoot   New stem growth

Simple fruit   Formed from one flower with one pistil and one ovary

Spores   Reproductive organs of non-flowering plants

Stamen   Male part of the flower—produces pollen

Staminate   Flower that produces only stamens

Stems   Organs that hold up plants and provide their basic shape

Stigma   Part of the pistil that receives the pollen

Stolons/Runners   Special stems that produce new plants

Stomata   Holes on the underside of a leaf

Style   Stalk of the pistil that supports the stigma

Succulents   Plants that have the ability to store large amounts of water

Taproot   One large central root with many smaller roots branching out

Taxonomy   Method of classifying living things

Tendrils   Special stems that grab onto things

Terminal bud   Bud at the end of a stem

Thorns   Special stems for protection

Tissue   Group of cells working together to perform a function

Tropism   Plant response to a particular stimulus/condition

Tubers and bulbs   Special stems that store food underground

Turf grass   Short grass used for lawns

Vacuole   Food storage location in a cell

Vascular tissue   Series of tubes similar to blood vessels for transporting nutrients and other chemicals throughout a plant

Vegetative reproduction/Vegetative propagation   Reproduction using part of the plant instead of seeds to start a new plant

Venation   Arrangement of a leaf's veins

Vine   Plants that grow on other plants or structures for support but have their own root systems

Whorled leaf arrangement   Three or more leaves grow from one node around a stem

Woody plants   Plants with stiff woody stems

Xylem   Tubes that transport water and nutrients from roots to the rest of the plant

Zoology   The study of animals

Challenge Glossary

Abiogenesis/Chemical evolution   Idea that at one time simple life came from nonliving chemicals; a modern version of spontaneous generation

Algin   Sticky substance found in kelp, a brown algae

Anaphase   Third phase of mitosis in which the chromosomes are pulled apart

Anthocyanin   Red or purple pigment in plants

Berry   Succulent fruit with multiple seeds

Bract   Bright colored leaf for attracting pollinators

Capillarity   Movement of water due to attraction of water molecules for each other

Carotene   Yellowish-orange pigment in plants

Carrageenin   Gelatin-like substance from red algae

Chemotropism   Response to chemicals

Cloning   Offspring have identical DNA to parent

Composite flowers   Collection of hundreds of tiny flowers on one stalk

Compound leaf   Several leaflets off of a single petiole

Crown   Branches of a tree

Cutting   Propagation by cutting a stem and stimulating it to grow new roots

Cytokinesis   The division of the cytoplasm

Deliquescent branching   Strong growth in lateral buds resulting in horizontal growth habit

Dichotomous key   Chart presenting two options at each level for classification

Diffusion   Movement of molecules from an area of higher concentration to an area of lower concentration

Disk flowers   Flowers comprising the head of a composite flower

Dispersing agent   External force aiding in dispersal

Double dormancy   Seeds require both scarification and stratification to germinate

Drupe   Succulent fruit with a single hard seed

Dry fruit   Simple fruit with a dry outer layer

Entire margin   Smooth leaf margin

Ephemeral   Plant with a very short life cycle

Epigeal germination   Cotyledons move above ground after germination

Epiphyte   A plant that grows on another plant using the host only for support

Excurrent branching   Strong growth in terminal buds resulting in a vertical growth habit

External dormancy/Seed coat dormancy   Dormancy lasts until seed coat is softened and/or broken

Fiddlehead   Developing petiole of a fern frond

Filament algae   Algae connected together end to end to form long stings

GMO   Genetically modified organism

Genetic modification   Modifying a plant's genes to obtain desired results

Glucose   Sugar produced in photosynthesis

Grafting   Propagation by combining a bud onto a rootstock.

Grain   Dry fruit of the grass family

Growth habit   Way the branches of a tree grow; a tree's shape

Head   Center of a composite flower

Hypogeal germination   Cotyledons remain below ground after germination

Internal dormancy/Embryo dormancy   Dormancy lasts until certain temperature or moisture requirements are met

Law of biogenesis   Life can only come from life
Leaf margin   The edge of a leaf
Legume   Dry fruit with a pod around the seeds
Lobed margin   Deeply indented leaf margin

Meiosis   Cell division that results in reproductive cells
Metaphase   Second phase of mitosis in which the chromosomes line up in the middle of the cell
Mitosis/Fission   Cell division resulting in two daughter cells identical to the original cell

Nectar/Pollen guide   Markings on flowers to direct pollinators to the nectar
Negative tropism   Movement away from the stimulus
Nut   Dry fruit with hard outer shell

Osmosis   Diffusion through a membrane

Peat   Layers of decaying peat moss
Pome   Succulent fruit with a papery core around the seeds
Positive tropism   Movement toward the stimulus
Primary growth   Growth that results in longer roots, stems, etc.
Prophase   First phase of mitosis in which the nuclear envelope dissolves

Ray flowers   Flowers that look like petals on a composite flower
Receptacle   Where the flower attaches to the stem
Root hairs   Tube-like projections on roots that are responsible for absorbing most of the water
Rootstock   Root and stem grown specifically for grafting

Scarification   Actions that result in breaking of seed coat
Scion   Stem or bud that is grafted onto a rootstock
Secondary growth   Growth that results in thicker roots, stems, etc.
Seed dormancy   Seeds will not germinate because certain conditions have not been met
Simple leaf   Only one leaf per petiole
Spines   Needle-like leaves designed to conserve water
Spontaneous generation   Belief that animals were suddenly produced by their surroundings
Starch   A string of glucose molecules linked together
Stratification   Seeds experience an extended period of cold temperature
Succulent fruit   Simple fruit with a thick fleshy outer layer
Succulent leaves   Fleshy leaves that store water
Sucrose   More complex sugar formed by combining two glucose molecules

Telophase   Final phase of mitosis in which nuclear envelopes develop around the chromosomes and cell divides into two separate cells
Thermotropism   Response to changes in temperature
Thigmotropism   Response to touch
Toothed margin   Jagged leaf margin
Transpiration   Evaporation of water from plants

Vascular bundles   Groups or bundles of xylem and phloem

Xanthophyll   Yellow pigment in plants

Zone of cell division   Region where cells are actively dividing
Zone of differentiation/Zone of maturation   Region where cells line up to form vascular tissue
Zone of elongation   Region of root that lengthens due to lengthening of cells

Index

Photo Credits